Lower West Side Story

Jack Foran

NFB Publishing
Buffalo, NY

Copyright © 2021 Jack Foran

Printed in the United States of America

Lower West Side Story/ Foran, 1st Edition

ISBN: 978-1-953610-56-0

1. Nonfiction> Murder>True Crime
2. New York State> Buffalo, New York
3. Religion>Catholic
4. Investigation> Crime> Cold Case

NFB
NFB Publishing/Amelia Press
119 Dorchester Road
Buffalo, New York 14213

For more information visit Nfbpublishing.com

For:

Oonagh,
Brendan,
Molly,
and Clare

And thanks to:

Dave Catalano,
Nelson Cosgrove,
Dick Donovan,
Terry Doran,
Larry Field,
Jim Kreuzer,
Michael O'Rourke,
Nancy Schiller,
and Dan Walsh

ONCE UPON a time a knight on horseback riding through a dark forest happened on a dwarf in the act of burying a great hoard of treasure in a pit he was digging at the base of a large tree. Jumping down from his horse, he caught hold of the dwarf—who sensibly did not put up any resistance to the superior might and weapons of the knight—and would have seized the hoard then and there and carried it off with him, but that it was so large he saw he would have to leave and come back with a cart to transport it to his castle. So still holding onto the dwarf, he made him promise to turn over the treasure to him, and not attempt to make off with it while the knight went off for a cart. The dwarf had to so promise. Meanwhile though, the knight could not just leave the treasure lying exposed on the ground, lest someone else find it and remove it. Whereupon, on the advice of the dwarf—who was a clever fellow—he determined to bury the treasure in the hole the dwarf had already made, and mark the location by tying a yellow scarf around the trunk of the adjacent tree. Though not before extracting further promises from the dwarf—for the knight was no fool either—not to tell anyone else about the treasure so that they might dig it up and remove it, or to remove the scarf from around the tree trunk.

The next day, when the knight returned with a cart and several companions to dig up and transport the treasure back to the castle, he found all the trees in that part of the forest—hundreds of trees—similarly marked with identical yellow scarves.

1.

GROWING UP Roman Catholic and of Irish ancestry and heritage in Western New York in the 1950s, you thought of the Church as Irish. If the Church was in any way an ethnic institution. For what you were taught officially in parochial school was that the Catholic Church was not peculiar to any ethnic or national group, that it was universal, which is what the word catholic means, universal. But the bishop, Joseph A. Burke, was of Irish ancestry. Like every previous bishop of the diocese, since John Timon, the first bishop of Buffalo, who arrived from Ireland in 1847. (The first non-Irish-ancestry bishop, Edward Kmiec, of Polish ancestry, was installed in 2004.)

The ethnicity of the bishop, like the ethnicity of the mayor, was significant of the general social standing and political authority—in the case of the bishop, a kind of higher-category political clout—of the relative ethnic community.

The mayors of Buffalo through the nineteenth century and most of the twentieth had been German or Irish. But beginning in the latter part of the nineteenth century, two new immigrant groups had arrived in Buffalo in large numbers, the Polish and the Italians. During the 1950s, by which time the Polish had become the largest ethnic group in the city, several mayors were Polish. But at the end of the 1950s, the mayor was Italian. Frank A. Sedita, the first Italian heritage mayor of Buffalo. It signaled the arrival—or a level of arrival—of the Italian community in the region.

WHEN TIMON arrived, in 1847, the population was mostly Irish and German. There were a few French—remnants of the much earlier era when the French contended for this corner of the New World for the water passageway it afforded into the heartland. But the French were fur traders and missionaries, not settlers, and never came in substantial numbers, the way other immigrant groups would. There was also a handful of Yankees, who had wandered in from New England on a general trek west in search of new pristine areas to exploit, and some of whom stayed on here. The French were Catholics. The Yankees were Protestant. The Germans, some of whom were Catholics, some of whom were Lutherans, were the first immigrants to arrive in numbers, though small numbers still in comparison with the other immigrant groups—including more Germans—that would show up over the next hundred years.

Then came the Irish. Or the first wave of Irish. Timon arrived one year before the official start of the Irish famine. So the greatest migration of Irish was still to come. But the economic situation in Ireland had always been difficult—at least for Irish Catholics—and Irish had been coming to America to find work since colonial times. The

Irish who came were Catholic. And even this first wave of Irish in Western New York must have outnumbered the German Catholics, or no doubt the bishop would have been German.

The first wave of Irish came to Buffalo in the aftermath of the construction of the Erie Canal, which was completed in 1825. The canal was dug—by hand—with picks and shovels—east to west, from Albany to Buffalo, by a small legion of Irish. So when the canal was completed, the Irish found themselves in Western New York, where many of them stayed to work on the docks and in the grain and lumber industries that would burgeon as a result of the transportation link here the canal created. Buffalo became the transshipment point—where cargo was transferred from one form of transportation to another—between Great Lakes shipping to and from the continental Midwest and barge traffic to and from the Atlantic coastal cities. And as railroads gradually replaced the canal, and Buffalo became the nation's second-largest rail center after Chicago, the Irish got jobs on the railroads.

When the Irish arrived, they lived on the city's Lower West Side, a wedge of territory between the Niagara River/Erie Canal, which formed Buffalo's western boundary, and roughly Niagara Street, which radiated north from the downtown commercial hub, and prominently included Canal Town, a notorious area of bars and brothels and slum housing centered on the canal terminus, where most of the Irish worked as day laborers on the docks. The proximity to Canal Town would have made the Lower

West Side a less than desirable residential district for more respectable portions of the community, that is, for families. But in the beginning at least there was little choice in the matter. The East Side—east of Main Street—was well settled already by Germans, who were establishment now, so that that was the fashionable part of town. The Irish couldn't have afforded to live there, even if they were welcome. Which they wouldn't have been. The Germans didn't particularly like the Irish. But then the Irish didn't much like the Germans, either. And the land to the north was remote from the port and the downtown commercial area, in addition to being prosperous farmland, and so probably not readily available for residential development. And the entire territory to the south was a Seneca Indian reservation, called the Buffalo Creek Reservation. But then in 1838 the state bought up the reservation, and the Irish relocated fairly en masse to the area, which would come to be known as South Buffalo, an informal designation for just another part of the city but with the cachet sense of a semi-autonomous area defined by the overwhelmingly Irish ethnicity of the population.

South Buffalo was also convenient to the steel mills, which came in about the year 1900, in Lackawanna, the territory just south of Buffalo, on the lake shore, and in the adjacent portion of South Buffalo. Many Irish worked in the steel mills, though the ethnic group most associated with labor in the steel mills—it had to be a new and particularly necessitous group to accept the extremely harsh and dangerous conditions in the mills—was the

Polish. Then later, the Blacks. The Polish lived in an area informally designated Polonia, on the remote East Side, not far from South Buffalo and the steel mills. This was a thoroughly Polish community, with even its own school system, a Catholic parochial system but operated not by the diocese but by the Polish parishes, and with instruction mostly in Polish. The Polish population, which clung tenaciously to its ethnic heritage, may have preferred it that way, but the separate school system was also a necessity, since neither the city public school system, overseen by the German-Yankee power structure of the time, nor the regular Catholic parochial school system, which had a thoroughly Irish cast, saw fit to build and operate schools for the Polish, who were considered suited and destined for one purpose only—to labor in the steel mills or some related brutish heavy industry. (After a worker's full term of employment in the steel mills, there wouldn't be much left of him. Moreover, accidental death in the mills was a regular occurrence in that era. For a while during the early years, there was on average one accidental death a day in the steel mills.)

The Blacks arrived in their greatest numbers in the first half of the twentieth century, and moved into the inner city areas of the East Side the Germans were moving out of now that these older areas were starting to deteriorate. The Germans could now afford more commodious living further to the east and in North Buffalo, which areas were now being developed residentially, and were favored as agreeably remote from the downtown business area hustle and bustle. And by the mid-twentieth century, the demographic spread—that is, white demographic spread—was to the suburbs.

AN ELEMENT of the Irish clung for a time to the Lower West Side, but by the end of the century, the area was being taken over by one of the newer groups, the Italians.

The Italians who came to Western New York were peasant stock for the most part, and worked in a variety of unskilled occupations, from agriculture to construction, to street peddling, with a predilection for outdoor work, if available. They competed for day labor jobs on the docks, but the Irish had the pick of that work. And perhaps due in part to a still vibrant and vital connection—poor and wretched as the Italian immigrants might be—to their substantial native cultural tradition—the art and architecture of the likes of Michelangelo and Leonardo, the music of Verdi and Puccini, the simpatico sense of connection to a benevolent, beneficent natural world of sun and rain and soil—the Italians by and large seemed to have had sufficient understanding of the true beauty and tragic brevity of life to reject the idea of spending a portion of this brief span in the quasi-inferno of the steel mills.

The Italians were also zealous for formal education—a characteristic no doubt also related to their historic cultural heritage advantage—and so made diligent use of public and parochial educational opportunities. And higher education, if possible, depending on personal or family financial circumstances. So that before long the

Italian community had notable numbers in the professions. By the early twentieth century, there were several dozen Italian lawyers and Italian physicians in Buffalo. Of the period substantial immigrant groups to Buffalo, only the Italians went about the business of upward mobility in the quickest, most efficient way, by securing as much education as possible. (Even as recommended by the Yankee and German power structure of the time for newcomers, a recommendation no doubt more calculated to obliterating what the establishment would have seen as offensive and suspect alien ethnicity than promoting the social and economic advancement of the new immigrant groups.) Whereas the Irish, in their excusable paranoia about sociopolitical Establishment counsel supposedly for their welfare and betterment, did not trust the power groups' recommendations. And the Polish would be forced to pull themselves up socioeconomically by their own bootstraps, which they would do eventually, but the process would take longer than in the case of the Italians. And any attempt at upward progress by the Blacks was spurned by white society in general, in a covert common effort to assure the continued presence of a socioeconomic sub-basement, as a guarantee that no white group, no matter how far it might descend down the socioeconomic ladder, into what hard times, would reach the bottom rung.

The Italians settled in several sections of the city, but mainly the Lower West Side, an area the Irish were then leaving of their own accord in a general exodus south, though the influx of Italians also helped stimulate the

Irish exodus. There were some turf wars, but the Italians seemed on the whole more determined, more tenacious, more steadfast even, than the Irish. They seemed to want to make more of a genuine community than the Irish. Canal Town was dying, but that too seemed largely related to the Italian influx. Canal Town was not the kind of community—or even suitable neighbor to the kind of community—the Italians wanted and were willing to tolerate. Canal Town was basically a service community to adolescent males (of whatever age). The Italian community was all about family, including children and old people.

The Italians also built churches. The Irish didn't have churches on the Lower West Side, but went to church to St. Patrick's, founded in 1840 and the second-oldest parish in the city, a short distance away, on Lafayette Square, where the Buffalo and Erie County Public Library now stands, and then to St. Brigid's, founded in 1859, in the First Ward, the portion of South Buffalo closest to the downtown commercial area and the docks. (The "mother" Catholic church of the region, St. Louis, founded by French settlers in 1829, but then soon afterwards taken over by the Germans, was a short distance uptown, at Main and Edward streets.)

Irish and Germans were also mainstay ethnic groups in the Cathedral parish when it started up in 1851. The Cathedral was and is on Franklin Street, west of Main Street, on what was called the Terrace, an embankment of higher ground separating and distinguishing downtown Buffalo from Canal Town and the Lower West Side. Initially, the

Italians went to church in an "Italian" chapel erected as an adjunct to the Cathedral proper about 1885 (likely more for the purpose of segregating the newcomers from the old guard Irish and Germans than to cater to the Italians). The "Italian" chapel is still a feature element of the Cathedral complex.

The first thoroughly Italian parish, established in 1904, was St. Anthony's, now just behind the present City Hall. Literally in the shadow of City Hall. The second, in 1906, was Our Lady of Mount Carmel, known as the Carmine, at Le Couteulx and Fly streets, streets that no longer exist, then in the heart of Canal Town. The first pastor of the Carmine was Irish, but after a few years an Italian pastor was appointed, the young and dynamic Father Joseph A. Gambino, who would in time become the patriarch of the Italian community in Buffalo, a man of indefatigable energy and zeal and even courage, as he proved when, on the occasion of a fire in the church, he went into the burning structure—against the advice and better judgment of the firefighters, who could not stop him, however—and rescued the consecrated eucharistic hosts from the tabernacle. The presence of the Carmine parish was probably more than any other single factor responsible for the eventual demise of Canal Town. As Father Gambino said once in a newspaper interview: "Where the police looked the other way, the Church wouldn't."

Following his success at the Carmine, Father Gambino was asked in 1914 to establish a new parish several blocks to the north, at Maryland and Seventh streets. The new parish, Holy Cross, eventually became the largest Italian-American parish in the United States outside New York City, numbering some 4,000 families, and including a parochial school, built in 1948, and even a Catholic movie theater, which operated for a while in the 1950s.

Holy Cross became the "mother" church of the Buffalo Italian community, having wrested that honorific from St. Anthony's now that St. Anthony's, situated as it was only on the fringe of the residential community, had become more of a "downtown" church.

Thus, the churches of the Lower West Side are Italian, and associated with the Italian community, not the Irish who were there before them, nor the Hispanic community that came after them (these days the foreign language Mass at Holy Cross is in Spanish). The Italians built the churches, and the churches and parishes became core vital social and religious elements of their community, much as Roman Catholicism was a core vital element of their cultural heritage.

So that what an Irish Catholic growing up in Buffalo in the 1950s would have missed—failed to understand—in thinking of the Church as Irish was that the Italians thought of the Church as Italian. With much better reason, based on historical fact and current culture. What the Irish Catholic would not have been fully aware of was the enormous pride the Italians took in the Church, the identification of the Church and the community, and sense of honor and pride derived from this identification.

MAYOR FRANK A. Sedita was a tremendously popular mayor. A kind of poor man's Fiorello LaGuardia (much as a later mayor, of Irish heritage, Jimmy Griffin, was a kind of poor man's Richard Daley). When Buffalonians who remember the middle of the twentieth century think back vaguely to the good old days, and think of who was the mayor, they probably think of Frank Sedita. He was a great politician—in the decent and honorable sense of that word—and perfect figurehead and standard-bearer for the ultimate achievement of status of the Buffalo Italian population.

2.

RUNNING IN Delaware Park—now it's the mid-1970s—I got to know and became friends with a runner who happened to be a Catholic priest, Father Dan Walsh. We had a lot in common. Basic Roman Catholic background, for one thing. And previously in graduate school I had studied medieval literature, and particularly Dante, which entailed substantial related studies of medieval philosophy and theology. Much the sort of things priests study in the seminary, though from a strictly theological rather than literary perspective.

Dan was just recently ordained then and wasn't yet regularly assigned to a parish but worked as a chaplain at one of the Catholic high schools. And summers, when he was free from his chaplain duties, he would be temporarily assigned to some parish to fill in for a priest or priests on vacation. One summer he was assigned to Holy Cross parish. And aware of my interest in all things Italian, he invited me to come and have a look around the church and the rectory, the priests' residence. He said it was a real interesting place.

So one Saturday morning, with nothing better to do, I ventured there. The place was pretty quiet. Dan was home, but the two or three other priests then assigned to the parish were gone for the day. Dan showed me around the rectory, an old Victorian semi-mansion with heavy, dark woodwork and furnishings. Pointing out items of interest. Including several artworks by one of the other priests living there at the time, Father Tom Ribits. Some paintings, and a collage of what seemed to be small found memorabilia, of the sort one might discover in an old desk drawer. Ticket stubs, a soiled, wrinkled photo, etc. Mementos, the point of which perhaps had been long forgotten. The point now, simply that they were mementos.

From the rectory, Dan took me into the church, through a passageway from the residence to the sacristy, the dressing room where the priest dons liturgical garb in preparation for Mass, and from the sacristy to the sanctuary, the railed-off area—as it always was in previous times—in the front of the church, where the altar is located.

The church was empty. On first impression, an odd-looking structure and space. A kind of tunnel nave with high wainscoting walls of creamy brown marble, and above the marble a strip of blue painted plaster wall blending seamlessly into the curve of a low arch ceiling of the same plaster material, the same color blue.

Dan pointed to the altar for my notice. The new altar,

that is, in the center of the sanctuary. In accord with the then-recent Vatican II decree that clarified the idea of the altar as a table on which the eucharistic meal was prepared by making it look like a table and turning it around so that the priest faced the people, the congregation, who were conceptually gathered around the table, sharing the eucharistic meal. Previously the altar was more an edifice monument against the back wall of the sanctuary, with niches and shelves for candelabra and flowers, so that the priest stood for most of the Mass with his back to the congregation. (In that early post-Vatican II period, when the new type of altar was installed, usually the old altar—because it was such a huge and prominent feature of the sanctuary that it would have been difficult as well as costly to remove it—was left in place, as it was in this instance. But also perhaps as a vestige of the old ways and so no doubt comfort to many of the congregation who were if not completely dismayed at least disconcerted by the Vatican II changes regarding modes and forms they had always considered immutable.)

Sometimes the new altar was simply a table on four legs, open underneath. Or sometimes the underneath open area was filled in with some artistic display item or material, such as a drapery hung across the front of the table, embroidered with some simple pictorial imagery, such as a eucharistic host and chalice, or maybe a scriptural phrase. But in this case, the underneath area contained a substantial artwork. A sculptural panel of abstract design in dark and foreboding shades of red-brown. A mosaic of myriad bits and pieces of some metallic material.

Copper or brass, perhaps. In a basic pattern suggesting the epicenter and surrounding centrifugal swirl form of some huge celestial manifestation. Cosmic phenomenon. Cosmic event.

Dan said to go up and look at the piece closely. Upon close inspection, I could see the panel was composed of bullet casings. A virtual honeycomb of small-caliber spent shells positioned on end, sometimes butt end outward, sometimes open end outward. Interspersed with primitive-looking square-profile nails. As if stamped from some matrix material low-grade iron. Dark, rusty-colored. But more bullet shells than nails, more brass than iron. A beautiful piece, visually and conceptually. About the act of creation, it seemed. Cosmic swirl of primal energy, exploding into matter. The violence of the initial creative moment. But also human violence. Sin. The bullet remnants. Instruments of violence. Transformed in an altarpiece as swords into plowshares. And the primitive nails reminiscent of the nails of the crucifixion. And so redemption.

Dan said it was by Tom Ribits, the artist-priest who made the collage and other artworks I had seen in the rectory.

AFTER THE sanctuary, we proceeded to the back of the church, where several tall stained-glass windows depicted various Italian saints, including most memorably St. Rocco, holding a little dish with two eyes in it. Patron of good vision, good eyesight, somehow. You pray to St. Rocco when you have an eye problem, or your vision is failing. In addition, in the vestibule was a small plaque commemorating a former assistant pastor of the parish, Father Vincent L. Belle, who had been murdered. A crime that remains unresolved.

On the other side of the vestibule was a large marble plaque and relief sculpture of Msgr. Gambino, founder and for many years pastor of the church, commemorating his long and distinguished service to the church and community.

I VAGUELY remembered the murder. Which occurred on New Year's Day of 1960. I was a freshman at Canisius College at the time. I remembered it as a major news event, but beyond that, didn't pay much mind to it. Something pretty remote from my college freshman world. I lived at home at that time on a farm in Clarence Center, an agricultural community well north of the city, and commuted to school. I remember I had the impression of guys I knew—Italians, from the city—being more connected to or affected by the event than I was. As something that related more to their community, not so much to mine.

BUT THINKING more about it, in the days and weeks afterwards, it dawned on me—I conceived—that the bullet casings altarpiece had to be somehow connected with the murder. As a kind of votive piece. An artwork as an act of expiation—atonement—a letting go of the bitterness and hardness of heart consequent on what would have been a communal psychic trauma. Swords into plowshares. The instruments of violence in the murder of Father Belle—

he was killed by a bullet or bullets—transformed into an artwork associated with the principal liturgical act of forgiveness and reconciliation, the re-enactment of Jesus' self-sacrifice on the cross.

But not just transformed—I began to think—but possibly also untransformed. Possibly somehow the altarpiece incorporated the actual shell or shells of the actual bullet or bullets that killed the priest. Revealed and yet concealed.

I BECAME curious about the incident, the murder. I went to the library and looked it up in the old newspapers on microfilm. I thought I might write something about it.

But it was very hard to understand. What happened. Why. I couldn't figure it out. The newspaper accounts were hard to understand.

For years, I kept going back to it, working on it for a time, then putting it aside. Trying and failing to understand. What happened and why. And why it was so hard to understand.

THE FATHER Belle plaque—the last time I looked—is no longer in the back of the church. (Maybe there never was a plaque. Maybe my recollection of the plaque is my memory playing tricks on me.) But in the years since, the vestibule seems to have been reconstructed, or refurbished. Nor are most of the Italian saints' windows still there. Rocco is gone. Of the windows I remembered from my first visit, only a St. Barbara is still in place. But now there is a small stained-glass window showing Father Belle in a bust portrait.

Neither is the bullet casings altarpiece still at Holy Cross. I don't know where it is now. But for years—later—when Father Ribits was a weekend assistant at St. Joseph's University Church in North Buffalo—it was there. At St. Joseph's, it was sometimes on display in the sanctuary. As an artwork, against the back wall of the sanctuary.

3.

EARLY ON the morning of January 1, 1960, the first day of the new year and new decade, Father Vincent L. Belle, a popular assistant pastor at Holy Cross Church, was shot and killed in his car in the church garage, as he was setting out to take Communion—the Eucharist—to shut-ins.

New Year's Day is a Church holy day. At that time it was called the Feast of the Circumcision, commemorating Jesus' circumcision. Father Belle helped distribute Communion at the 7 o'clock Mass at Holy Cross that morning, then went to his car to visit and take Communion to the sick of the parish. But some time later, after some of the families of the sick who had been expecting his visit called the rectory to inquire as to his whereabouts, and he did not return in time to say the 9 o'clock Mass he was scheduled for, so that another assistant, the Rev. Francis J. Zuech, had to substitute for him, the pastor, Msgr. Gambino, sent another assistant, Father Anthony J. Caligiuri, to go look for Father Belle, presumably by driving around the neighborhood and looking for his car. When Father Caligiuri got to the garage, he discovered Father Belle's lifeless body in his—Father Belle's—car.

The murder was not immediately discovered, however. There were no obvious signs of violence, and it was supposed that Father Belle had suffered a heart attack. Though he was only 38 years old, he was somewhat overweight. He was 6-foot 5-inches tall, but weighed 230 pounds. Father Caligiuri administered last rites, and a physician was called from nearby Columbus Hospital, who upon arrival officially pronounced Father Belle dead. The body was then removed to a funeral home where during mortuary preparations several bullet holes were found in Father Belle's torso and left arm. The mortician immediately notified the police and the Erie County medical examiner, who ordered an autopsy.

BUFFALO HAD two newspapers at the time, the *Courier-Express*, a morning paper, and the *Evening News*. The story came out in both papers the next day, Saturday, January 2. The *Courier* broke the story, under an eight-column front page banner headline: "Buffalo Priest Slain in Garage," and a two-column three-line stacked subhead: "Police Lack Clues; Crime Shocks City." Also on page one was a three-column picture of Father Belle's car and a police homicide detective looking it over, a head shot of Father Belle, and no less than seven sidebar stories in addition to the main story, which ran long on page one, then jumped to page three. One of the sidebars also jumped to page three. Also on page three, in addition to the two story continuations, was another picture, of Father Belle at his first Mass. The picture, from June 1, 1947, is a particularly dramatic one: the handsome young priest, tall and quite slim at that time, at the poignant moment of just ascending the altar steps, flanked by two other priests—Mass servers—kneeling. Father Belle's hands are folded in prayer at his chest, his eyes are closed—at least at the split second of the photo—in an attitude that looks to be something between reverential meditation and ecstasy, as he is caught in mid-step, head and shoulders bowed slightly forward, the alb—liturgical full-length white gown-like, lace-trimmed garment—flowing gently rearwards at the bottom. So that he almost seemed to flow or float the few steps up to the altar.

The servers are identified in the caption as the Very Rev. Msgr. Francis J. O'Connor and the Rev. Francis P. Sorci. The caption explains that Msgr. O'Connor, who was then, in 1960, the editor-in-chief of the *Union and Echo*, the diocesan weekly newspaper, in 1947, when the photo was taken, was a seminarian at Christ the King Seminary, St. Bonaventure University. And that Father Sorci, who in 1960 was the pastor of Our Lady of Mt. Carmel Church in Angola, was a lifelong close friend of Father Belle.

ONE OF the *Courier* front-page stories was an appeal by the police for tips. Police Commissioner Frank N. Felicetta was quoted saying that all information would be kept confidential. The story said this was the only case in the 112-year history of the Diocese of Buffalo of a murder of a priest.

The other sidebar stories included:

A statement by the Catholic Bishop of Buffalo, Joseph A. Burke, who said: "We of the diocese are depressed as well as shocked by the loss of such a saintly priest." Noting that the priest was en route to parish homes to deliver Communion, he said Father Belle "died in the line of duty." Bishop Burke said he was as mystified as the police by the murder. He also said—probably in response to a question from a reporter—that the chancery had not had sufficient time to consider the advisability of offering a reward for information in the case.

A statement by the Episcopal Bishop, Lauriston L. Scaife, who saw the case as an argument for improved social services. "If the tragic and needless killing of a member of the clergy points up the care of our citizenry both psychiatrically and rehabilitationally," he said, "then it will have served some purpose. But it is a terribly expensive experiment."

A statement by Dr. Joseph L. Fink, rabbi emeritus of the city's main Jewish temple, Beth Zion, who lamented that "when the community reaches a level where the lives of the clergy are endangered, it is a serious situation." He added that "when innocent men like [Father Belle] are attacked, it is a reflection on the general character of the community."

A statement by Mayor Frank A. Sedita—said to be a parishioner at Holy Cross Church—who said Father Belle was "one of the finest men I have ever met in my life." He said the news of Father Belle's death was "a terrible shock to me. I wish I were able to say why it happened."

Reactions of various other parishioners, who "all spoke highly of the dedicated priest." This long sidebar story jumped to page three.

Another sidebar noted the sad fact that Dr. Rocco Di-Dominicis, the county medical examiner, who was called to the scene because of the unusual nature of the death, but initially failed to discover the criminal aspect, had also been the attending physician at Father Belle's birth, thirty-eight years before.

THE FRONT-PAGE main story in the *Evening News* the same day ran under the banner headline: "Press 3-Way Hunt in Priest's Slaying," and two two-column three-line stacked subheads: "Homes Canvassed, Records Studied, Weapon is Sought," and "100 Officers Seeking Clues; Assistant Pastor of Holy Cross Slain in Garage Ambush." Also on page one was a head shot picture of Father Belle, and three sidebar stories. And the main story jumped to page 4, where there were four more stories, and a picture of Commissioner Felicetta and Homicide Bureau Chief Harry G. Klenk looking over Father Belle's car in the garage.

One of the front-page sidebars, under the headline "Can You Help Solve Murder?" reiterated Felicetta's appeal for confidential tips from the public. Next to the appeal for information was a sketch map of the layout of the parish buildings and vicinity—the area delimited by Niagara, Maryland, and Seventh streets. Niagara and Seventh run parallel, connected by Maryland. The church is on Maryland, at the corner of Seventh. The rectory is behind the church, attached to the church, on Seventh. The garage is behind the rectory, unattached. At the corner of Niagara and Maryland at that time was Holy Cross School, and on Niagara, next to the school, was the Catholic Theatre. Holy Cross parish ran its own commercial cinema for several years around this time. It showed movies—as an alternative to the standard commercial fare that was becoming a cause of alarm to Catholics and others concerned about a perceived general moral decline—that would have been approved and promoted by Church officials. (The main feature at the time at the Catholic Theater—according to ads in the movies sections of the papers—was "The Sheepman," starring Glenn Ford and Shirley MacLaine. The second feature was "Andy Hardy Comes Home," starring Mickey Rooney.)

THE ACCOUNTS in the two papers agreed in most details. There was no sign that this was a burglary or robbery gone awry, since no money or property seemed to have been taken or disturbed. And there was little likelihood of mistaken identity of the victim, as Father Belle was physically such a big man, and well-known and well-recognized in the community. Apparently, there was some early thinking that the victim might have been mistaken for the manager of the Catholic Theater, one Blase Palumbo, who had permission to park in the rectory garage. However, Mr. Palumbo was only about 5 foot 7 inches tall and weighed about 140 pounds, so it was unlikely he would have been mistaken for Father Belle. (It is not reported what Mr. Palumbo might have thought of the initial speculation that he was the intended victim.)

The car was dusted for fingerprints, but no strange prints were found. No weapon was found, and police were combing area backyards, alleys, and garbage cans for a .32-caliber handgun. The slugs retrieved from Father Belle's body were .32-caliber. Ballistics tests were being performed on the slugs to determine whether they were fired from a revolver or an automatic. No shells were found in the car or on the garage floor. (A revolver would not have ejected shells. But if the bullets were fired from an automatic, which would have ejected the shells, it meant the gunman must have stopped and picked them up before leaving the scene.)

There were some small discrepancies in the two papers' accounts. For example, in the matter of who discovered the body. The *Courier* said it was Father Caligiuri. The *News* said it was Father Caligiuri and Father Zuech.

Another discrepancy concerned Father Belle's precise position in the car. The *Courier* said Father Caligiuri found Father Belle "upright in the driver's seat. His head was tilted backwards." Whereas, the *News* quoted Father Zuech, who said, "We found him lying on his right arm, on the right side of the seat."

Elsewhere in the *Courier* story, a possible scenario of the murder is presented—said to be based on detectives' theories—that actually comports more with the *News* version that Father Belle was slumped across the front seat, and suggests why the bullet holes were in his side, under his arm. In the *Courier* scenario,

Father Belle climbed into his car, leaving the left door open. He put the ignition key into the lock. Then, with his left arm resting on the steering wheel, he leaned over to the right and placed a vial of holy oil—to be used on his visits—in the glove compartment.

The gunman stepped close to him at that moment and fired three rapid shots from a few inches away.

One shot struck the priest in the lower chest. Two more plunged into his arm, one of the two passing through the arm and into the left chest. The bullet holes were only three inches apart.

Dr. DiDominicis, who issued the certificate of homicide, said the two bullets that entered the body traveled at an upward angle and lodged in the upper right chest, near the armpit. "Death was so quick there was no external bleeding," he said. The close-range shots left powder burns on the priest's black cloth jacket. These looked like faint dust smudges, so that the shooting initially went undetected.

The *News'* reconstruction of the scene was similar to the *Courier's*, except that the *News* said Father Belle placed a prayer book in the glove compartment, rather than a vial of holy oil.

Both papers mentioned—in each case with no further explanation—that a 55-year-old West Side man had been brought in Friday afternoon for questioning, and then released. Police did not give the man's name or indicate why he might have been detained. The *News* also said three other people had been questioned at police headquarters.

No motive for the murder was determined. "It looks like the work of a fanatic," District Attorney Carman F. Ball was quoted as saying, in both papers. In their search for the killer, which was described as one of the most intensive manhunts in the history of criminal investigation in Buffalo, it was said that police compiled a list of runaway patients from area mental hospitals. The *News* said one of the persons who was questioned had been discharged recently from Buffalo State Hospital, the primary local institution for the mentally ill. (Episcopal Bishop Scaife's statement—on the need for psychiatric and rehabilitational social services—reflected a similar notion to the district attorney's that the murderer might have been a deranged person. This idea seems to have quickly gained currency among the investigators and reporters working on the case.)

There was speculation that Father Belle might have known the killer. For instance, that it might have been someone he was counseling about some personal or domestic situation. Police were checking Father Belle's correspondence and other papers for the name of someone who might have conceived some grudge against him.

Though based on the reactions of parishioners, Father Belle had been a very highly regarded as well as popular figure in the community.

Carmen DiPaolo, a past president of the parish Holy Name Society, said, "a great saint of the church has died." He said, "there is no question but he was the greatest man I or anyone could be associated with. He was an outstanding priest…his love knew no bounds."

Mrs. Mary Gugino, president of Holy Cross Home and School Association, said, "Father Belle was a wonderful man. I don't think a better priest could be found anywhere."

Another parishioner, Joseph Nasca, speculated that the killer "would have to be insane." He said, "Father Belle was a saint. There wasn't a better man living. The children loved him. My two daughters are broken-hearted."

The *Courier* noted that the church pastor, Msgr. Gambino, who was 82, was deeply shocked at the incident and had retired to his quarters and was unavailable for comment. The *News* said Msgr. Gambino, overcome by stress following the murder of his assistant, had been placed under a doctor's care and given sedation.

One of the stories in the *News* said the murder was the topic of conversation throughout the Lower West Side. The paper said everyone had a theory, but "the consensus seemed to be, as the police said, that a fanatic or psychopath committed the crime."

ANOTHER FRONT-PAGE story in the *News*, running beside and below the Father Belle story, reported that Massachusetts Senator John F. Kennedy formally announced his candidacy for the Democratic Party presidential nomination.

Senator Kennedy said he was entering the New Hampshire primary, to be held in March, and would enter other primaries that he did not want to specify at present.

In making the announcement for the presidency, the senator said he "would not be a candidate for vice-president under any circumstances, and that is not subject to change under any conditions."

4.

THE DILIGENT police work paid off. The Sunday (Jan. 3) *Courier* reported that on Saturday night a 77-year-old West Side man, Alfonso Catalano, who apparently had felt some grievances against Father Belle, was arrested and charged with first-degree murder.

The page-one story was accompanied by a picture of Catalano at police headquarters being escorted by a detective. Small of stature and slight of build—the top of Catalano's head came up to about the detective's chin—with white hair and metal-frame glasses and baggy trousers, he seemed in the picture a little bewildered at all the fuss and goings-on, but not particularly concerned.

Sidebar stories—no doubt developed prior to the information on the arrest—said the *Courier* was offering a reward of $1,000, and an anonymous person was offering a reward of $500, for information leading to the arrest and conviction of the killer. The *News* did not publish on Sundays.

Catalano, who the *Courier* said had several aliases—Dominic Carolina and Dominic Carlina—was described as a retired laborer and widower and the father of four children. The exact nature of his supposed grievances against Father Belle was not revealed. However, it was said that the suspect was linked with a "crude threatening message directed at Father Belle" that had been tacked to a door in the vestibule of Holy Cross Church two weeks before.

The message was said to be in Italian and painted in black paint, partly in block letters and partly in longhand, on a one-foot-square piece of sheet metal. The paper said the message "accused Father Belle of 'improper conduct' and warned him to discontinue the practices imagined by the writer." The message did not mention Father Belle by name, but referred to "the long man," which the *Courier* said was "interpreted from the Italian" to mean Father Belle, who was six-foot, five-inches tall.

The *Courier* said Msgr. Gambino "said he discussed the threatening message with Father Belle after it was found and was satisfied the charges were completely unfounded."

In addition, "Msgr. Gambino said the posting of the message was preceded by an anonymous telephone complaint containing the same fancied allegations. The monsignor said he received the phone call a few days before the message was posted."

Nor did Police Commissioner Felicetta put any stock in the allegations against Father Belle. According to the newspaper account:

> Felicetta said the accusations against the priest were "strictly the figment of imagination" and "there is no reason to believe Father Belle's conduct was anything but impeccable."

POLICE SAID a search of the suspect's apartment turned up a piece of sheet metal from which the one-foot-square piece apparently had been cut. They described the discovery of the matrix sheet as the "first big break" in the case.

Police were led to the suspect by an anonymous tip received by Commissioner Felicetta. The tipster said the suspect had owned a gun and had been known to make disparaging remarks about a priest. However, under intense questioning, the suspect repeatedly denied any involvement in the matter, and repeatedly denied owning a gun.

Despite the denials, Felicetta called Catalano a "very good suspect" in the murder. Police pointed out that Catalano had a police record dating back to the 1930s for traffic violations, and in 1938 he had served 30 days in jail for operating a still.

Because the suspect was illiterate and incapable of writing the threatening message himself, the police were checking his acquaintances in the belief that someone else wrote the sign for him.

The paper said Catalano was a Holy Cross parishioner and attended the 7 o'clock Mass daily, and the morning of the murder he had received Communion from Father Belle, who helped distribute the sacrament at the 7 o'clock Mass, just before he left for his rounds to shut-ins, when he was killed. The paper said initially Catalano said he attended only the 7 o'clock Mass the morning of the murder, but confronted by statements of other parishioners, admitted returning to the church for the 9 o'clock Mass. The suspect was picked up outside his home Saturday afternoon.

Police said the search for the gun was continuing in homes, alleys, and trash cans on the West Side. Felicetta said he could not recall "such a large concentration of effort" for one case in the 30 years he had been with the police department. He said more than 100 policemen were working on the case, some of them coming in on their days off, one even returning from sick leave to help out.

Ballistics test results indicated that the bullets had been fired from a revolver, in which case, no shells would have been ejected. Police had noted that none were found on the floor of the garage or in the car.

IN ADDITION, the *Courier* interviewed Msgr. Gambino. He said Father Belle's work "especially with the sick at home and in hospitals, distinguished him as one of the top servants of God." He said Father Belle had been "a gentle, kind, and thoughtful priest," and "there was only goodness, and humility in his manners, work, and personality." The monsignor confessed he was puzzled by the incident. "It is not easy to understand why a person would want to harm a priest," he said. "I am an old man and he was always considerate. He was such a good man and so very young. I cannot understand this."

The story noted again that Msgr. Gambino was under a doctor's care and had been given sedation following the discovery of the murder.

IN ADDITION to the $1,000 reward for information offered by the *Courier*, and the $500 reward offered anonymously, Erie County 11th Ward Supervisor Frank E. Wendling said he would ask the county Board of Supervisors the following week to post a $5,000 reward for information leading to the arrest and conviction of the murderer.

Commissioner Felicetta, who had announced the anonymous $500 reward, said he was sworn to secrecy as to the identity of the donor. He said the donor was a professional man, and "a very close personal friend of Father Belle," as well as a friend of the police commissioner. He said the donor was not a parishioner, and that the donor would be consulting with him—Felicetta—in deciding who should receive the reward.

IN A follow-up story on Senator Kennedy's announcement the day before for the Democratic nomination for president, Kennedy challenged other aspirants to the nomination to enter state primaries.

Other possible aspirants included Senator Hubert H. Humphrey of Minnesota, Senator Stuart Symington of Missouri, and Senate Democratic Leader Lyndon B. Johnson of Texas. Kennedy said in making his decision to run, he accepted former Illinois Senator Adlai Stevenson at his word that he would not be a candidate. Stevenson had been the unsuccessful Democratic nominee for the two previous elections.

In reply to questions, Kennedy conceded that his Roman Catholic religion was likely to be a "matter of substantial discussion in the campaign." But he thought it would be "of less interest to the voters than the politicians."

5.

THE MONDAY (Jan. 4) Courier said an unnamed West Side woman had come forward with a story that seemed to explain Catalano's supposed grievance against Father Belle. She said Catalano had conceived a romantic interest in her, a married woman with eight children, and when she rejected his romantic advances, he imagined she "was spurning him in favor of Father Belle."

In addition, an eye-witness had come forward and identified Catalano as the man he had seen run out of the garage behind Holy Cross Church around the time of the murder. The eye-witness said he heard the man exclaim, in Italian, "God, what did I do!"

The paper said the West Side woman had contacted police following the shooting and "revealed that Catalano had an 'imaginative grievance' against Father Belle." To Commissioner Felicetta, the woman's story, in conjunction with other known facts and circumstances, seemed to confirm the "fanatic" theory, and even suggest a likely crime scenario. The relevant portion of the *Courier* account is as follows:

> The woman told police Catalano, a long-time friend of her husband and herself, had forced his attentions on her. She repeatedly had brushed him aside, explaining she was a happily married woman with eight children.
>
> She said that for some unexplained reason, Catalano accused Father Belle of interfering in the suspect's efforts to gain her love. The elderly man had mentioned this to her in conversation when she refused to go out with him.
>
> She further revealed that on New Year's night, about 10 hours after the murder, Catalano approached her, showed her a small revolver, and warned her to "keep quiet about this or I will kill you."

"Several weeks ago," Felicetta said, "the woman's husband contacted police to tell us Catalano had come to him to inform him that she had been intimate not only with Father Belle and another priest, but also with three doctors in a hospital clinic where the woman had gone for treatment.

"This strengthens positively that this man imagined the whole matter and that it was a figment of his own imagination and his own jealousies.

"I believe the killer met the priest as the latter was walking to the garage, and the killer, fanatic in his ideas, probably made his complaint in person to Father Belle," Felicetta said.

"The priest, although likeable and gentle, also was a big, strong man who, if he had wanted to, could easily have disarmed the killer. However, Father Belle was carrying the Holy Sacrament with him, and a priest cannot make any conversation—nor even speak a word—while carrying the Host.

"The priest probably ignored the killer and got into his car. This would have vexed the killer even more and, for this reason, the man fired at Father Belle as he sat in the car ready to turn on the ignition."

Following his arraignment, Catalano was to be taken to Meyer Memorial Hospital for tests to determine his sanity.

A front-page picture in the *Courier* showed detectives searching among ceiling rafters at Catalano's residence with a mirror-on-a-pole device and a flashlight, looking for the "death weapon," the picture caption said. The story said police also used "a mine detector" to search Catalano's yard, where neighbors said they had seen Catalano digging of late. But still no gun was found.

BY ODD coincidence, apparently, the woman's husband—the man who told police Catalano had told him his wife was intimate with Father Belle and another priest and three doctors in a hospital where she had gone for treatment—was the man police had initially questioned. This information was first revealed Monday afternoon in the *News*.

The *News* published earlier and later editions Monday, with different front-page stories on the murder. Moreover, the later edition had an inside-page mostly recap story on salient details of the case and the police theory, including a number of items that had previously appeared in the *Courier*. (The *Courier* had published two days' papers—Sunday and Monday morning—since the previous *News* issue.)

The *News* early-edition story pretty much reiterated the *Courier* story, that Catalano, some hours after the killing, had showed the woman a small pistol and told her: "Keep quiet about this or I will kill you." But omitted the information about Catalano allegedly having told the woman's husband that his wife and Father Belle were romantically involved, but merely said that Catalano "blamed Father Belle for her coldness toward him."

The *News* early-edition story did not say where the confrontation with Catalano occurred—when he supposedly showed the woman a pistol and threatened her—but said it "happened Friday evening, when the woman's husband was not at home," and that "she reported it to Commissioner Felicetta in a telephone call Saturday."

THE *NEWS* later-edition front-page story provided further details on the confrontation, including where it occurred—on the street—and a somewhat different threatening quote. Also, the information that the woman's husband had initially been a suspect, and information about a domestic dispute some time previous between the woman and her husband in which Father Belle had intervened, resulting in a call to police and the husband being taken in for questioning. According to the *News* later-edition front-page story:

> The woman told police that New Year's evening—Father Belle had been killed that morning—she went to a neighborhood store with one of her children.
>
> They were returning home when a car pulled alongside them at Busti and Maryland St., only a block from the murder scene.
>
> Catalano, the driver, leaped out and rammed the muzzle of the pistol against her stomach. She quoted him as saying:

"Do you want to die here or do you want to die at home?" The woman said she had known before that Catalano had a gun, but he never carried it on the street and she was terrified.

She said he freed her only when she promised to let him drive her and her child back to an out-of-city school to which the child is returning after the holidays.

Ironically, the woman's husband was first considered a possible suspect in Father Belle's murder.

Some months ago the priest was in the neighborhood when the sounds of a domestic struggle were heard in the street outside.

At the request of neighbors, he intervened and called Niagara Station police. The woman's husband was taken to the station for questioning, but no charges were placed.

The paper said, "Her story is an integral part of the police case against Catalano because it establishes a motive for the bizarre killing—Catalano is said to have blamed Father Belle for the woman's attitude toward him—and because it places him in possession of the type of weapon which killed the priest."

The paper said Police Homicide Chief Harry Klenk said the woman had taken three lie detector tests and the police accepted her story fully.

THE *NEWS* later-edition recap story talked about the telephone call to Msgr. Gambino and the sign posted in the back of the church accusing "the long man" of improper conduct, and threatening to report the matter to no less a Church authority than the Pope. But said "the monsignor conferred with Father Belle and the two other assistant pastors, then dismissed the matter as the product of 'a warped mind.'"

The story said "Commissioner Felicetta believes Catalano's actions in the church bear out the theory that jealousy and emotional strain over a period of months had gradually turned Catalano into a fanatic." As to the woman's story that Catalano was pursuing her and blamed Father Belle for her rejection of him, the later-edition recap piece said her story "is borne out by a complaint which her husband made to police several weeks ago. He said Catalano accused his wife of improper conduct with Father Belle, another priest, and three physicians…"

Meanwhile, Catalano continued to deny any connection with the crime. "Lapsing from broken English into Italian," the *News* early-edition story said, "Catalano steadfastly denied the killing during 12 hours of police grilling Saturday night and early Sunday." The later-edition story noted that "Catalano's home is only a few minutes' walk from the Niagara River, and police fear the gun may have been thrown where it will never be found."

BOTH PAPERS said the eye-witness—one Rudolph Avellino—told police he saw Catalano run from the garage behind Holy Cross Church, across Seventh Street, and through the Public School No. 1 schoolyard, sometime between 7:20 and 7:25 a.m. the morning of the murder, and heard him say, in Italian: "God, what did I do!" The *News* story noted that Avellino had not heard any shots.

(Oddly, the seemingly very significant information on the eye-witness appeared in the *Courier* buried deep in the long main story on the investigation, then in the *News* only at the bottom of the recap story, possibly indicating suspicion generally as to the reliability of the eye-witness and his allegation, particularly given that the eye-witness had apparently come forward after the notice of reward money was posted in the Sunday *Courier*.)

SEVERAL OTHER people told police they saw Catalano in the vicinity of the church and/or the garage the morning of the murder, before 7 o'clock and after.

Both papers reported that Catalano had received Holy Communion twice that morning—at the 7 o'clock Mass and again at the 9 o'clock Mass—and that this was a violation of Catholic Church law. Both papers noted that Church law allows Catholics to attend Mass as often as they wish, but permits reception of Communion only once a day.

ABOUT A dozen police officers conducted a basement-to-attic search of the suspect's home—Catalano had made no objection, and a family member supplied a house key—involving tearing up floorboards and using a mirror-on-a-pole device and flashlight, as pictured in a *Courier* photo, to search between floor and ceiling joists for the murder weapon.

The search of the house turned up a .32-caliber cartridge, which the *News* described as "similar to the three that killed the Rev. Vincent L. Belle."

THE NEWS gave a fuller report than previously on Catalano's previous arrests. The paper said his record went back to 1921, when he was charged in the City of Buffalo with burglary and grand larceny counts that were later dismissed. And in 1937 he was sentenced to 30 days in jail, and in 1938 to five months in jail, on federal charges of operating a still. Similar charges laid in 1934, 1938, and 1940 were ultimately dismissed. In addition, the paper said Catalano had been charged with a number of traffic counts, and that in each of the Buffalo arrests he had refused to sign the arrest card, contending that he was illiterate.

THE MONDAY *Courier* showed a head shot of Catalano looking calm and smiling, as if blissfully unaware of the predicament he was in. Or perhaps it is a picture from a previous, happier time, though he seems to be wearing the same checked shirt and sweater as on the previous day in the picture with the detective, following his arrest. (He showed no signs of distress in that picture, either.)

The Monday *News* showed a different picture of Catalano, a head shot of him scowling and disdainful, tousled hair, sans glasses, as if in the aftermath of the intense grilling both newspapers had referred to. So the worse for wear, and possibly fully cognizant at last of his grim situation.

MSGR. GAMBINO had been hospitalized for hypertension and angina, due to shock and stress in the wake of the murder of his assistant pastor. He had been at the rectory Saturday where he greeted mourners, but on Sunday was admitted to Sisters Hospital on the advice of a physician. He was listed in fair condition, and was expected to remain in the hospital a week.

The Most Rev. Leo R. Smith, Auxiliary Bishop of Buffalo, was to substitute for Msgr. Gambino at a children's Mass scheduled for 8:30 a.m. Tuesday, prior to the funeral Mass scheduled for 10 a.m.

REV. RAYMOND G. Bosch, a professor of modern languages at Canisius College, where Father Belle had studied prior to entering the seminary to study for the priesthood, said the Sunday noon Mass at Holy Cross and eulogized the slain priest in his homily.

"Who can say anything against Father Belle?" Father Bosch asked rhetorically. He likened the "murderous assassin" of the young priest to Cain, who "rose up against Abel his brother and slew him," and compared Father Belle's death to that of Jesus Christ on the cross. Like our Savior, Father Bosch said, Father Belle died "a martyr for God." He told the congregation: "Do not pray for him, but pray to him, for his intercession."

The papers said the church was full to capacity, with parishioners standing in the side aisles and at the back. Other parishioners queued up outside the rectory, waiting to pay their respects to Father Belle, whose body lay in state inside.

Mayor Sedita—a parishioner—attended the noon Mass and helped take up the collection.

*   *

SOME OF this is hard to see. Hard to grasp. For example, Felicetta's statement in the *Courier* that the husband's story about Catalano telling him his wife had been intimate with Father Belle and other men "strengthens positively that [Catalano] imagined the whole matter and that it was a figment of his own imagination and his own jealousies." On the premise perhaps that Father Belle was a saint on earth. Without flaw or foible. Which however seemingly was indeed a premise of this investigation. Recall Felicetta's statement from the get-go (*Courier*, Jan. 3) in this regard:

> Felicetta said the accusations against the priest were "strictly the figment of imagination" and "there is no reason to believe Father Belle's conduct was anything but impeccable."

Or the unattributed statement in the *News* later-edition recap that the woman's story about Catalano pursuing her and thinking Father Belle was interfering in that illicit romantic project was "borne out by a complaint which her husband made to police several weeks ago. He said Catalano accused his wife of improper conduct with Father Belle, another priest, and three physicians…"

MOREOVER, DO the husband's story—about Catalano telling him his wife was intimate with Father Belle and three other men—and the woman's story—about Catalano pursuing her romantically and wanting to marry her—even seem to logically accord, comport?

MEANWHILE, THE woman's story becomes the basis for the identification of Catalano as a fanatic, consonant with the police and prosecution theory that Father Belle's killer had to be a fanatic, given that Father Belle was such a good man, so there could be no rational motive for his killing.

Or was the basis of the fanatic theory the sign in the back of the church and phone call accusations—both apparently by Catalano—of improper conduct by Father Belle? Accusations summarily dismissed by Msgr. Gambino as "the product of a 'warped mind,'" as well as by Commissioner Felicetta, who believed that "Catalano's actions in the church bear out the theory that jealousy and emotional strain over a period of months had gradually turned Catalano into a fanatic."

IN ADDITION, we learn—indirectly from the *Courier* story—that there was a clear motive for someone else to have killed Father Belle. Namely, the husband, who believed or may have believed Catalano's story that Father Belle was having an affair with his wife. Why wasn't that angle explored?

THEN IN the *News* later-edition front-page story, we learn that it was. Or at least was discussed. "Ironically, the woman's husband was first considered a possible suspect in Father Belle's murder."

But then the story doesn't say why. That is, doesn't make the connection to the glaringly obvious reason, that Father Belle may have been having an affair with his wife. Or at least that he may have thought so. Which we know from the *Courier* that morning.

> "Several weeks ago," Felicetta said, "the woman's husband contacted police to tell us Catalano had come to him to inform him that she had been intimate with Father Belle and another priest, but also with three doctors in a hospital clinic where the woman had gone for treatment."

Whereas, the *Courier* story does not say that the man was considered a suspect. And neither the *News* early-edition story or later-edition front-page story says about the husband telling police what Catalano told him about Father Belle and his wife. Only the News later-edition recap story mentions that interesting item (reported that morning in the *Courier*). But off-handedly, and as if by way of confirming—as if to confirm—the woman's story that Catalano was pursuing her romantically and had a grudge against Father Belle for interfering in his romantic intentions. "The woman's story is borne out by a complaint her husband made to police several weeks ago. He said Catalano accused his wife of improper conduct..."

FINALLY, THE seeming incongruity between the information in the *News* early-edition front-page story that the confrontation between the woman and Catalano the evening of the day of the murder—when he showed her a gun and threatened her—occurred "when the woman's husband was not at home," and the later-edition front-page story statement that the confrontation happened on the street, at the corner of Busti and Maryland streets. The earlier information—that it happened when the husband was not at home—seemed to imply that it happened at the couple's home. But it didn't. So what was the relevance of this information? About the husband not being home at the time?

6.

THE TUESDAY (Jan. 5) papers reported the arraignment of Alfonso Catalano, 77, of 549 Busti Avenue, Buffalo, on a first-degree murder charge. During the procedure, Catalano was said to mutter repeatedly, in Italian, "I don't know anything about it."

Defense Attorney Morris Lipsitz entered no plea, but objected to the charge on the grounds that the main supporting affidavit, from Rudolph Avellino, the alleged eye-witness, was not properly attested. Presiding Judge Joseph P. Kuszynski overruled the objection.

Mrs. Josephine Mercurio, a county probation officer, translated the accusation into Italian for the defendant. Attorney Lipsitz also objected to the use of the interpreter, on the grounds that no plea was being entered. Once again, Judge Kuszynski overruled.

NO SUBSTANTIAL new developments were reported in the investigation. Police Homicide Chief Harry Klenk told the papers he had learned that Catalano had owned guns for many years, though without a permit. He said police had also learned the suspect had recently acquired a new gun. They thought this gun might have been the murder weapon.

The gun still was not found, however, and the search for it continued. Police said the previous night they had questioned several close friends of the suspect on the matter.

7.

THE WEDNESDAY (Jan. 6) papers—and two days later the diocesan weekly *Union and Echo*—told of how Father Belle was laid to rest in the priests' lot at Mount Calvary Cemetery following a requiem Mass at Holy Cross Church, Bishop Joseph A. Burke presiding.

About 1600 mourners attended the funeral Mass, including numerous clergy and civic leaders, among them Mayor Sedita. Other mourners unable to get into the packed church stood outside.

There was no homily, but at the end of the service Bishop Burke stood for a few moments at the open bier and said silent prayers for the slain priest, then blessed the body, whereupon all the priests present also gave blessings.

The *Union and Echo* listed the priests who assisted at the Mass. Among these, Father Francis Sorci, who was in the picture in the *Courier* several days earlier from Father Belle's first Mass. Father Sorci was designated archpriest of the funeral Mass. The paper said he was an assistant at St. Lawrence Church when Father Belle was growing up in that parish, and they had remained lifelong close friends.

Msgr. Francis O'Connor, the other priest shown in the *Courier* picture from Father Belle's first Mass, was not listed for the funeral Mass (but his name appeared on the masthead of the *Union and Echo*, where he was then editor-in-chief).

The *Union and Echo* said that about 200 of the laity received Holy Communion at the funeral Mass, which the story described as "a relatively new practice that has started in the diocese." Prior to about that time, Communion was not usually distributed at funeral Masses.

POLICE CONTINUED their search for the missing gun, checking manholes in the area around Catalano's home with electromagnetic instruments. The *Courier* noted that underworld figures sometimes hid firearms in manholes. It was the only reference in the papers to the underworld—aka Mafia—in connection with the murder. Around this time, references to the Mafia were often challenged by anti-defamation crusaders, who claimed the Mafia, which was a secret organization, did not exist. Terms such as "underworld" or "organized crime" or "mob" were used instead of Mafia.

8.

THE MURDER trial of Alfonso Catalano got underway July 1, 1960, in Erie County Court. The final jurors had been selected the previous day. At that time, the newspapers printed names and addresses of jurors, and even religious affiliation, if deemed relevant. In this case, the all-male jury was said to consist of eight Protestants and four Catholics.

Visiting County Judge Maurice W. McCann, who usually was assigned to neighboring Wyoming County, was to preside.

IN HIS opening remarks, District Attorney Carman F. Ball laid out the prosecution theory that Catalano killed Father

Belle because he thought the priest was interfering with his unsuccessful romantic pursuit of a woman whom Ball identified as Mrs. Mary Congilosi, 49 years old, married, and a mother of eight. Ball said Catalano "in his mind got to suspect something was going on between Father Belle and Mary Congilosi."

Ball said that initially, following the death of Catalano's wife four years previously, Catalano had proposed marriage to Mrs. Congilosi's mother, Mrs. Gelorma Amato, a widow in her eighties, but had been rejected. Whereupon, Ball said, he turned his attention to the daughter, who also spurned his advances. He said Catalano wanted Mrs. Congilosi to divorce her husband and marry him. Ball noted that one of Father Belle's pastoral duties was as a marriage counselor in the parish.

Ball said one of the prosecution exhibits would be a sign that appeared on the bulletin board of Holy Cross Church, written in Italian, appealing to the parishioners to "go to the Pope" about "the long one." This was taken to refer to Father Belle, who he said was 6 foot 4 inches tall. Ball said there would also be evidence that Catalano had phoned Msgr. Gambino, the pastor at Holy Cross, where Father Belle was assigned, and "asked him to get rid of Father Belle."

DEFENSE ATTORNEY John W. Condon in his opening remarks said the prosecution's evidence was circumstantial and did not meet the test of legal proof. When Condon tried to impugn the credibility of Rudolph Avellino, the alleged eye-witness, the prosecution objected that this was not a proper part of an opening statement. Judge McCann sustained the objection. Judge McCann also sustained an objection to Condon's assertion that some prosecution witnesses might "have reason to color" their testimony.

As opposed to the idea that Catalano was romantically interested in Mrs. Congilosi, Condon said there was "an excellent reason" for the long-standing friendship between Catalano and the Congilosi family.

Condon noted that Catalano was 77 years old and a regular church-goer, and had successfully raised four children. He said the defendant was "more interested in meeting his Creator in the twilight of his life than in romance."

THE FIRST witnesses included three physicians and an undertaker. Dr. John Mosijczuk, a physician from Columbus Hospital, was the first to examine Father Belle in the garage where he died, and although the death seemed to be due to natural causes, because Father Belle had previously been in good health, he called in Erie County Medical Examiner Dr. Rocco DiDominicis. When Dr. Di-Dominicis arrived about an hour later, he concurred with Dr. Mosijczuk that Father Belle had died of natural causes, and authorized removal of the body to a funeral home.

Funeral Director Anthony P. Amigone testified that at the funeral home, after he had removed the priest's upper clothing, including a black coat, he noticed what he said "appeared to be bullet holes" in the upper body. He at once notified Police Commissioner Felicetta and Dr. Di-

Dominicis, and the body was taken to Meyer Memorial Hospital for an autopsy. Amigone said he had seen no blood on any of the priest's outer clothing.

Dr. Edward G. Eschner, from Meyer Memorial, testified concerning the autopsy. He said three bullets were found in the body, two in the chest and one in the upper left arm.

THE NEXT witness was Msgr. Joseph A. Gambino. On direct examination by District Attorney Ball, Msgr. Gambino testified that at the time of the slaying he knew Catalano by sight, but had never talked to him. However, he said, around the middle of December 1959, about two weeks before the murder, he received a telephone call from someone who, speaking in a Sicilian dialect, made accusations against Father Belle. Following the murder and Catalano's arrest, Msgr. Gambino said he talked to Catalano for about ten minutes in the county jail. The *News* reported the following exchange between Msgr. Gambino and Ball.

> "Did you recognize the voice of the man you heard on the telephone?" asked Mr. Ball.
>
> "I did," Msgr. Gambino replied.
>
> "Whose voice was it?" asked the prosecutor.
>
> "Alfonso Catalano," Msgr. Gambino testified…
>
> "The man on the telephone conversed in the Sicilian dialect," Msgr. Gambino testified. "He

told me that 'prato longo' – meaning Father Belle – was a bad priest and to get rid of him. I told him this was a very serious accusation, and to come to the rectory to talk things over.

"The man said on the phone that Father Belle was leading a double life, one life that of a priest, and the other keeping company with a woman."

(*Note: The form "prato," for "prete," the Italian word for "priest," in Msgr. Gambino's testimony, is surely a misinterpretation by the reporter. It is not anything a speaker of Italian or an Italian dialect would likely have said. A later newspaper report refers to the words on the sign as "prete longo," translatable as "tall priest.")*

MSGR. GAMBINO testified that when a parishioner told him about a sign posted in the vestibule of the church, he had the sign brought to him. He said the message was on a piece of tin about 18 inches square. Msgr. Gambino said he later—presumably after the murder—turned the sign over to the police.

As to who made the sign, Msgr. Gambino said he did not think Catalano had written the words on it, because "he wouldn't know how to write them." He said he thought the words had been written by "a man now dead." He did not elaborate.

In a puzzling exchange during cross-questioning, Condon asked Msgr. Gambino if, following the murder, "someone in authority" had requested that he not discharge Mrs.

Congilosi from her job in the Holy Cross School cafeteria. The *News* said, "Msgr. Gambino testified he could not recall whether Mr. Ball made the request."

9.

FATHER ANTHONY J. Caligiuri, an assistant pastor at Holy Cross, testified that on January 2 at police headquarters he overheard a conversation in Italian between Catalano and Mrs. Congilosi, in which Mrs. Congilosi said: "Why don't you tell them the truth? Tell them what you did with the gun. It will be easier for you if you tell them everything." To which he said Catalano responded: "Why don't you keep quiet? Don't tell them anything. They don't have anything on us."

Defense Attorney Condon vigorously objected to this testimony, but was overruled. Condon argued that a more accurate report of the conversation could be provided by police officers investigating at that time. Judge McCann did allow objections to Father Caligiuri's testimony on conversations between Catalano and Mrs. Amato, the mother of Mrs. Congilosi, whom Catalano was said to have courted before turning his attentions to Mrs. Congilosi.

TIMOTHY McLAREN, a student at Canisius College and the fiancé of Miss Phyllis Congilosi, daughter of Mrs. Congilosi and her husband, Alphonse Congilosi, testified that Catalano had told him he was "going to shoot" Mr. Congilosi, and also was "going to get those priests" and "that priest."

McLaren said he was a frequent visitor in the Congilosi home, at 290 Busti Avenue, where he said Catalano also frequently visited, based on Catalano's lifelong friendship with Mrs. Congilosi's late father, Mr. Amato.

McLaren said Catalano, who owned a car, sometimes drove him from the West Side to Canisius College, a distance of a few miles across the city, and that on one of these occasions, in November 1959, Catalano told him:

> "Mrs. Mary Congilosi, mother of my fiancée, was a good woman and he was 'going to shoot' her husband, Alphonse Congilosi.
>
> "Catalano told me he was going to shoot Mr. Congilosi in the cellar of his house," Mr. McLaren testified. "Then he went on to say he was going to get those priests, and then he was going to get that priest. He said to me, 'You wait and see.' He called me 'Big Boy,' and I said, 'You are watching too many television programs.'"

Ball asked if Catalano appeared to be serious in saying these things, and McLaren said he did. Condon objected to this exchange, but was overruled.

PHYLLIS CONGILOSI then testified that in the fall of 1959 she heard Catalano tell her father: "'I'm going to kill you. You don't deserve your good family and good children. If I were in your place I'd be very happy…" She said "then there was a lot of screaming and yelling."

She said Catalano also told her: "'I'm going to kill your father. He doesn't deserve your mother.'" She said Catalano told her "he wanted to take her father's place because her mother was 'a good woman and my father didn't appreciate her.'"

District Attorney Ball asked her: "What was the main source of discord between your father and mother?" She said: "Mr. Catalano."

MRS. CONGILOSI'S sister, Mrs. Angeline Swier, testified that Catalano had a gun that, after Father Belle had told him to stay away from Mrs. Congilosi, he threatened to use on Belle. Both papers reported Mrs. Swier's testimony at length. From the *News* account:

> Mrs. Swier testified that Catalano threatened to kill Father Belle after the priest had told him to stay away from Mrs. Congilosi…
>
> "Sometime before last Thanksgiving Day, I happened to see a gun sticking out of Catalano's pocket when he came to my home. We were in the kitchen and I asked him if the gun was a real one.
>
> "He said he never went anywhere without a gun. He said he had never used the gun, but wasn't afraid to do so.

"I saw him again sometime later and he said he had dropped his gun and a son-in-law had destroyed it. He said the gun fell and his son-in-law picked it up and banged it on the floor and it broke.

"After last Thanksgiving he came again to my home and took out a different gun and banged that one on the kitchen table. He told me my sister was meeting Father Belle and he said he was going to write the Pope about it.

"He also said she was having an affair with three doctors, a lawyer, and a priest, and he was going to get even with all of them. Whenever my sister went to see a doctor, he assumed she was having an affair."

"Did the defendant ever say he wanted to have an affair with your sister?" John W. Condon Jr., defense attorney, asked on cross examination.

"No," Mrs. Swier replied.

"He said only that he wanted to marry her?" asked the defense counsel.

"Yes," Mrs. Swier testified. Mrs. Swier testified that her sister has eight children, the youngest 17.

In answering questions by District Attorney Ball, Mrs. Swier testified she told Catalano to remember that to kill Father Belle "would be a sacrilege and a mortal sin because he (Father

Belle) was the cloth of our Lord."

Mrs. Swier testified that Catalano replied "he had a way of doing it."

She testified that Father Belle always left the church on his rounds of sick calls at a definite time and that the priest always carried the Sacrament with him.

She testified that Father Belle always warmed his car before starting to leave the garage.

"What next did he say?" asked Mr. Ball.

"He said when Father Belle comes back, that is when he is going to tell him to either leave Mary and him alone or he would kill him. Then he told me he would kill Father Belle so no one would hear the shots. He told me that he would throw the gun in the sewer. He told me he would hide it."

*   *

SOME BITS of comic relief amid the murder trial solemnities. In the semi-hilarious portrait of the braggadocio gangster, who boasts he always carries a gun, but when somebody bangs it on the floor, it breaks. And Timothy McLaren's advice to Catalano when Catalano threatens to kill Mr. Congilosi and several priests to boot, that he had been watching too much television.

And in the *Courier* account of Mrs. Swier's testimony,

after the talk about killings and throwing the gun in a sewer, she says Catalano said he would "get a good lawyer who would spring him."

But intimations as well that all is not peace and harmony in the Congilosi family. Suggestions of serious family discord—possibly not entirely of Catalano's instigation—raising doubts about Mrs. Congilosi's statement about being "happily married."

10.

THE PURPORTED eye-witness, Rudolf Avellino, testified he saw Catalano follow Father Belle into the garage behind the church, heard three shots, saw Catalano exit the garage, and heard him say: "Oh God, what did I do?" The *News* account is as follows:

> Mr. Avellino, who, Mr. Ball said, is unemployed, testified he spent New Year's Eve visiting a number of taverns in the downtown area, and finally walked from Chippewa and Franklin streets to Maryland and Seventh streets, across from Holy Cross Church.
>
> "Did something attract your attention as you arrived at Maryland and Seventh streets?" Mr. Ball asked.
>
> "I got there about 7 a.m. and I saw a person

near the church garage," Mr. Avellino testified.

"Who was that?" asked Mr. Ball.

The witness pointed to Catalano, who was sitting in front of the courtroom with his counsel.

"Then I saw Father Belle coming out of the rectory and walk into the garage," Mr. Avellino continued. "I heard Catalano hollering at him."

John W. Condon Jr., defense counsel, objected to the word "hollering" on the ground it was a characterization of what Catalano allegedly said. He was sustained by the court.

"Father Belle just pushed Catalano aside," Mr. Avellino testified. "Then Father Belle got into his car and Catalano walked into the garage."

"Then what happened?" asked Mr. Ball.

"I heard three shots," Mr. Avellino testified.

"Were you in a position where you could look into the garage?" asked Mr. Ball.

"Yes," the witness testified.

Mr. Avellino testified that after the three shots were fired, Catalano left the garage and crossed the street to where he was standing. He said that Catalano said something in Italian to him, but he could not give an accurate translation into English.

Mr. Avellino said Catalano then said something in Italian which he could identify.

"Catalano said as he passed me, 'O Deo! Chi Fieci,'" Mr. Avellino testified.

"What does that mean in English," asked Mr. Ball.

"God, what did I do?" Mr. Avellino testified before a hushed courtroom audience.

At this point, Judge McCann ordered a short recess.

FOLLOWING THE recess, during cross-questioning, Avellino admitted he had lied in January in sworn statements to the district attorney and the grand jury in that he said at that time he had not heard any shots. (A *News* story in January noted that Avellino had not heard any shots. Nor was there any indication in the papers in January that Avellino had been able to see into the garage.)

Avellino said he hadn't mentioned the shots before last month, because up until then, he said, "I was scared." He also admitted during cross-questioning that in January when he came forth with his eye-witness information he was facing Federal Court sentencing on a series of check thefts, and that there was at that time an outstanding warrant for his arrest on a charge of assaulting his estranged wife. And he admitted to another assault on his estranged wife, the day before New Year's Day.

When Condon tried to question him regarding the source of his income the previous year, and specifically whether he had been employed by the police as an "informer," the judge advised him of his right to invoke the Fifth Amendment. (He may have done so. No further details are recorded on the matter.)

SOME OBVIOUS questions about the trustworthiness of this witness and his testimony, based on his changed testimony from what he told authorities in January, and regarding his Federal Court problems, which giving testimony might conceivably mitigate. Also the blatant incorrectness of the quoted Italian, raising doubts about what he allegedly heard and/or understood. In particular, "chi" does not mean "what," it means "who." "What" would be "che." Some other noteworthy solecisms in the four-word quotation: "Deo" for "Dio," and "fieci" for "feci." Possibly dialect forms, or possibly misquotes by the *News* reporter. But suspicious.

In addition to doubts about his reliability in that he only came forward with his eye-witness account after rewards were offered for information on the case. The reward offers were posted in the Sunday (morning) *Courier*. The *Courier* and *News* stories about Avellino as eye-witness were in their Monday editions. (The *News* stories omitted mention of rewards, however, particularly since one of the reward offers was from the *Courier*, and to mention rewards would require mentioning the *Courier*. The *News* did not offer a reward.)

*　*

THE DAY Avellino testified—Monday, July 11, 1960— was the opening day of the Democratic National Convention in Los Angeles. The day before—Sunday, July 10—

the Rev. George E. Stauffer preached at Parkside Lutheran Church on the topic: "Political Conventions and God's Intentions," wherein he considered the question whether a Roman Catholic could be an impartial president. The Monday *Courier* reported on the sermon at length, as follows:

> The Rev. Mr. Stauffer said:
>
> "Should a man's affiliation with the Roman Catholic Church automatically bar him from serving his country?
>
> "All of us would answer emphatically, 'No.'
>
> "Roman Catholics have served ably as American soldiers, jurists, senators, governors, and in every political capacity except president and vice-president.
>
> "Why then do some of us question their ability to fulfill their duty in this highest office in the land?
>
> "Because their Roman Catholic religious scruples may hamper them in serving their fellow Americans impartially.
>
> "Would you select a Quaker to be our Secretary of Defense? A Christian Scientist to be our Secretary of Health? A Jew to be the American ambassador to Egypt?
>
> "To say that a man can be president without listening to his conscience or his religious upbringings is a dangerous assertion. It is the

Roman Catholic's experience in a church that many of us consider undemocratic and intolerant which frightens the Protestant at the prospect of having a Roman Catholic in the White House," the pastor continued.

"It is a fact of history—not a tenet of theology—that in countries where Roman Catholics are in the majority—Italy, Spain, Mexico, Columbia [sic], Argentina, Portugal, and a host of others—there is absolutely no religious toleration of Protestants."

The 35-year-old pastor said that while no citizen should vote against any candidate simply because the candidate is a Catholic, each voter might properly ask himself three questions:

1. "Would a Roman Catholic yield to the political pressure of the most powerful church in the world and break some of his specific pre-nomination promises concerning the separation of church and state?"

(Earlier, the pastor quoted Sen. Kennedy's strong affirmation of his belief in separation of church and state and his opposition to federal funds for parochial schools.)

2. "Would a Roman Catholic be able to fulfill the function of his political office at non-Catholic religious ceremonies when his church says specifically that it is a sin to attend such services?

3. "What would happen to American foreign

policy, for example, in countries which desire birth control information to answer their population problem when the Roman Catholic might make this a religious issue rather than an economic one?"

11.

A WOMAN testified that she and her husband drove to Holy Cross Church about 5:15 or 5:30 a.m., January 1, 1960, hoping to be able to attend Mass, and saw a man she now identified as Catalano standing in the driveway between the church and the school.

She said she and her husband had entertained in their home New Year's Eve. She said Holy Cross Church was dark, however, so they drove on to St. Anthony's to see if there was a Mass there at that time, but found the Mass at St. Anthony's almost over. So they drove back to Holy Cross. She said the man was still standing in the driveway, and she rolled down the window and asked him when Masses were at the church. She said he shrugged his shoulders and told her the church was closed.

Another woman testified she saw Catalano in church at the 7 o'clock Mass and saw him leave before the end of the Mass, as soon as Father Belle had finished helping distribute Communion.

CITY POLICE Detective Michael A. Amico testified about conversations he overheard at police headquarters between Catalano and Mrs. Congilosi, and Catalano and Mrs. Amato, Mrs. Congilosi's mother. The *News* account of Amico's testimony is as follows:

"Mrs. Congilosi asked Catalano to co-operate with the police and tell him [Detective Amico?] where the gun was hidden," Detective Amico testified. "Catalano said to her: 'Why are you talking, keep quiet, keep your mouth shut.'

"Mrs. Congilosi told Catalano that the police 'are trying to incriminate me. I want you to tell the truth, tell them where the gun is.'

"In reply, Catalano said: 'Why, you police stool pigeon, you tattler—keep your mouth shut.' Then Catalano told Mrs. Congilosi he had kept his mouth shut, and if she would keep quiet, 'they won't have anything on either of us.'

"Mrs. Congilosi told Catalano she just wanted the truth to be known, and again asked him to tell about the gun. She urged him to aid the police and said the police would help him out."

Detective Amico testified Mrs. Amato also urged Catalano to co-operate with the police. He said she told Catalano to admit he attended 9 o'clock Mass in the church, pointing out that she had seen him in the church at that time.

"Mrs. Amato said: 'You were there. I know. I

received Holy Communion with you at the altar rail. Why are you lying to the police? Why don't you tell them the truth? You are telling them that you didn't go to the 9 o'clock Mass and that you went to the 7 o'clock Mass.'

"Catalano responded by asking Mrs. Amato: 'What difference does it make?'" Detective Amico testified.

*   *

INDEED, WHAT difference could it make? This line of inquiry—as to whether Catalano attended both the 7 and 9 o'clock Masses—recalls the hobbyhorse irrelevance matter in the January papers about Catalano possibly having received Holy Communion twice in one day.

BUT WHAT is strange and most puzzling about the conversation between Catalano and Mrs. Congilosi at police headquarters is her supposed remark that the police were "trying to incriminate" her. There had been no overt—or plausibly even covert—suggestion of incrimination of Mrs. Congilosi. If she said that—that the authorities were trying to incriminate her—possibly it was to try to get Catalano to confess, if she could make him think she might end up taking the fall if he avoided it. Or possibly it represents some sort of psychological transference—whether conscious or unconscious—of a fear of possible incrimination of Mr. Congilosi. Possibly Mrs. Congilosi was trying to protect Mr. Congilosi. (Or protect herself, by protecting Mr. Congilosi.)

*   *

DETECTIVE AMICO later became Erie County Sheriff, but is perhaps best recalled in local historical memory as the police official behind the attempt to pin drug charges on renowned University of Buffalo literary scholar Leslie Fiedler. That was in 1967, when Amico was still with the Buffalo Police, where he had risen to chief of the Bureau of Narcotics and Intelligence. It was an era of hysteria over a spectrum of social and political issues, most prominently, of course, the Vietnam War, and Fiedler had recently accepted the faculty advisor position—apparently because no one else would take it—for a university student group that advocated legalization of marijuana. Amico's bureau had kept the Fiedler house under 24-hour surveillance for 10 days prior to the arrest, and then equipped a 16-year-old young woman guest at the house with an electronic transmitter that allowed police to monitor conversations in the home, prior to entering the house and searching and locating some marijuana and hashish in a third-floor bedroom. Fiedler was charged with "maintaining a premise" where narcotics were used. He was convicted of the charge in a Buffalo court, a conviction that was later overturned by the New York State Court of Appeals.

12.

HOMICIDE DETECTIVE Albert Vingoe testified that at police headquarters he overheard Catalano say, in a kind of Shakespearean soliloquy, it would seem, "I wish the Good Lord would strike me dead for the awful thing I've done." Vingoe said he had just finished questioning Catalano, when Catalano sat down and began to "talk to himself."

Defense Attorney Condon objected to testimony about the defendant's alleged conversations with himself, but was overruled.

MRS. CONGILOSI then testified. She said that on New Year's Eve, prior to the murder of Father Belle, Catalano confronted her on the street, pointed a gun at her, and threatened her. And on New Year's day, following the murder that morning, he visited the Congilosi home twice during the day, and in the evening confronted her on the street again, and threatened to kill her and her family and himself as well. (Previous accounts had only mentioned one street confrontation, following the murder.) She said also that Catalano had once given her a revolver in a restaurant. The fuller account of her testimony was in the *News*, as follows:

A mother of eight children testified Wednesday in the Alphonso Catalano murder trial that the defendant threatened to kill her and her family New Year's Day.

Mrs. Mary Congilosi, 290 Busti Ave., a prosecution witness, added that Catalano once gave her a revolver to keep for him while they drank coffee in a restaurant at Main and Virginia Sts.

She testified in English and Italian after Dist. Atty. Ball engaged Mrs. Antonina Vella, 179 Plymouth Ave., to interpret conversations Mrs. Congilosi had with Catalano in Italian.

Mrs. Vella, a teacher 14 years in the University of Buffalo, speaks both Italian and the Sicilian [sic].

Mr. Ball told County Judge Maurice W. McCann he wished Mrs. Congilosi to tell the exact words used by Catalano, rather than interpret them in English. John W. Condon Jr., defense counsel, objected to this form of direct examination, but the court overruled him.

Mrs. Congilosi said she has known Catalano 20 years because he was a friend of her late father and mother. Mrs. Gelorma Amato, Mrs. Congilosi's mother, died [the previous] Friday [July 8, 1960].

The witness testified that, shortly after her father's death, four years ago, Catalano began to woo her mother.

"I have loved you for 20 years, but I haven't been able to approach you because your husband was my best friend," Mrs. Congilosi testified Catalano told her mother. "My mother told Catalano that her husband was freshly buried. She refused his advances."

Mrs. Congilosi then explained that she met Catalano on Maryland St. New Year's night, some 12 hours after the Rev. Vincent L. Belle had been found shot to death in the garage at the rear of Holy Cross Church.

She testified Catalano told her: "This time I'll really kill you, your husband, and everyone in your family—then I'll kill myself."

She added that Catalano, in previous conversations with her, had accused Father Belle of "putting ruin between us" when she repulsed his offer of marriage and his inducements to divorce her husband.

"On New Year's night, Catalano said to me: 'They can't do anything to me. I am old. I have good lawyers, they can't do anything," Mrs. Congilosi testified. "He told me that, if I should tell, he would kill everyone in my family. The night before, on New Year's eve, I met him as I was going home from the store.

"Catalano approached me with a gun and pointed it at my side. He asked me: 'Do you want to die here or in the house?'

"I said, you can kill me here or where you wish, just so you don't do it in front of my son, who will become even more ill than he is. He then blamed me for taking advice from 'the long one.'"

Mrs. Congilosi explained that a son is mentally retarded, and earlier witnesses testified that Catalano called the priest "the long one" because Father Belle was more than 6 feet tall.

She added that, in August 1959, Catalano drove her several times a week to Buffalo General Hospital, where she was under outpatient treatment. She testified that one occasion they stopped in the restaurant at Main and Virginia Sts. for coffee. She said he told her he had a revolver and she warned him it was against the law.

"Catalano told me, better put it in my purse while we were in the restaurant or he might get picked up by the police," Mrs. Congilosi testified. He told me: "I feel bare without a revolver. With a revolver, I can do anything. Whenever they want something done, they call me. They are all my friends."

Mrs. Congilosi noted Catalano did not explain who "they" are. She said she put the weapon Catalano had in his pocket in her purse and "when we got out of the restaurant, I gave it back to him.

"Just before Christmas in 1959, Catalano asked me to leave my husband and said he would keep me like a queen. I told him that God blesses a woman with but one husband and, even if he is bad, she has to keep him.

"Catalano said that if my husband wasn't good to me, he had a good lawyer to get a divorce and that it would not cost me a cent."

She testified Catalano came to her home twice New Year's Day, at 11 a.m. and 2 p.m. She said she had heard about Father Belle's death from a woman friend and told Catalano about it.

"Did Catalano ever make advances to you?" Mr. Condon asked on cross-examination.

Mr. Ball objected on the ground the word "advances" has several meanings, and Mrs. Congilosi explained that Catalano wanted to marry her "so he could take care of me."

Continuing his cross-examination, Mr. Condon obtained an admission that the witness had called police after Catalano had threatened her New Year's night.

"When he threatened to kill the whole family, I was scared. I had to do something about it," Mrs. Congilosi explained.

Additional information in the *Courier* story included that in the 11 a.m. encounter with Catalano in the Congilosi home, when Mrs. Congilosi told him Father Belle was dead, she said his response was, "He didn't give a damn."

UNDER FURTHER cross-examination, Mrs. Congilosi testified, in the *News* version, that her husband was "'jealous of everybody, including priests,'" and had "threatened to kill her and three of their children with an axe." The more extensive *Courier* version of this testimony is as follows:

> "He was jealous of everybody," she said.
>
> "Was he jealous of the priests?" Condon asked.
>
> "Yes," she answered.
>
> Mrs. Congilosi then was asked whether she recalled her husband saying to her that if he ever found her being unfaithful with a priest, he would kill "both of you."
>
> "He said that if he ever found me being unfaithful, he would kill me, but not anybody else," Mrs. Congilosi answered.
>
> The witness said she did not remember telling anyone at the Holy Cross School cafeteria on the day of Father Belle's funeral, "That's the last time my husband will have to worry about my cheating with Father Belle."
>
> Mrs. Congilosi said Father Belle was visiting the family above her flat last fall or winter, when her husband struck her. She said Father Belle told her, "You don't have to take that." She also admitted that last Oct. 28 her husband threatened to kill her and three of their children with an ax.

Mrs. Congilosi testified her husband was at home on the morning Father Belle was shot. She said he did not attend Mass on New Year's Day, even though it was a holy day of obligation.

SO IT turns out the initial suspect—a man with a comprehensible motive, who said he was told, and apparently believed, or at least suspected, or may have suspected, his wife and Father Belle were romantically involved—was jealous and abusive and threatened mayhem violence.

(Strangely, Mr. Congilosi's threats are essentially similar to the threats Mrs. Congilosi related in her story of the street encounter—now become encounters, plural—with Catalano, sometimes to kill just her, sometimes to kill her and her children as well. Possibly another case of psychological transference.)

13.

THE METAL sign that had been posted in the back of the church was entered as evidence.

The *News* provided the legend in the original: "Padre Gambino, mantiene il prete quello longo con la namorata—Al Papa rivogetevi." Mrs. Antonina Vella, the University of Buffalo Italian instructor consulting for the court, translated this as: "Father Gambino maintains the priest—that long one—with sweetheart—Turn to (or have recourse to) the Pope."

Mrs. Vella said most of the words in the message were proper Italian, but some were in Sicilian dialect. "There is no Sicilian language," she explained, "but a Sicilian with some formal education could have written it."

(Note: The word "rivogetevi" must have been "rivolgete-vi," to make sense and in accordance with the way Mrs. Vella translated it.)

IN ADDITION, police who had searched Catalano's home testified they found a large piece of sheet metal there, and believed the metal for the sign had been cut from the larger piece. And a police chemist said he tested the ink used on the sign, and said in his opinion it was of the same type as ink found in Catalano's home.

The paper noted that Mrs. Swier—in testimony several days before—had said Catalano at one point had told her he was going to write a letter to the Pope, and had asked her how to spell the Italian word for "long." (The Italian word for "long" is "lungo," meaning in this case "tall." But longo, close enough.)

RECALL THAT the message on the sign was generally characterized in newspaper stories in January as "threatening." It is hardly threatening, unless an advisement to have recourse to the Pope is considered threatening. But hardly threatening in the primary and usual sense of the term of threatening harm, the sense seemingly intended in the newspaper stories.

14.

POLICE COMMISSIONER Felicetta testified that "the husband of a main prosecution witness charged the defendant with having told him that his wife was too friendly 'not only with Father Belle, but also with Msgr. Gambino.'" There were "audible gasps of amazement" at the mention of Msgr. Gambino in this connection, the *News* story said.

> "Mrs. [an apparent typo for Mr.] Congilosi told Catalano in my presence and in the presence of his wife that 'you told me she was fooling around, not only with Father Belle, but Msgr. Gambino and three doctors at the hospital where Mary was taking her treatments,'" Commissioner Felicetta testified.
>
> "Catalano then told Mr. Congilosi to 'keep his mouth shut or he would kill him too,' and called him in Italian a stool pigeon and police informer."

Felicetta said Mrs. Congilosi also was brought to headquarters to confront the defendant. According to the *News* account:

When Mrs. Congilosi appealed to Catalano "to get the thing off his chest, the police would help him if he came clean," Catalano told her, the commissioner testified, to "keep her mouth shut, the police had nothing on him, and it would be better for all concerned."

IN CROSS-EXAMINING Felicetta, Condon asked him about a time a police officer showed Catalano a revolver partly hidden in a towel and told him police had found the gun he had used in the murder. According to the *News* story:

> ...Felicetta said that Catalano "looked at the officer and said: 'No, you didn't. You haven't found any gun. Don't be kidding me.'"
>
> "Is that a kind of ruse, to get an admission?" Condon asked.
>
> "I suppose," the commissioner conceded, "it could be called a trick of some kind."
>
> Mr. Condon drew an admission from the police commissioner that the 77-year-old widower had "never admitted" the slaying of Father Belle.

Asked who would get the $500 reward money put up by an anonymous donor, Felicetta said he had not decided. From the *Courier* account:

"Do you mean to say," Condon asked, "that [Rudolph Avellino, the purported eyewitness,] will not get it?"

"I don't know," Felicetta said. "I can't say. I don't know who is entitled to it."

Condon then attempted to show that Avellino knew about the $1,000 reward offered by the *Courier* and the $500 by an anonymous donor when he first came forward with his information. Felicetta said he was certain Avellino didn't know about the $500 reward when he came forward. Condon then asked, "Is Rudolph Avellino a police informer, a stool pigeon?" "He's never been an informer of mine," the commissioner said.

15.

"TO BOLSTER the testimony of Rudolph Avellino," as the *Courier* put it, the prosecution called Victor Leto, a friend of Avellino who joined him on part at least of his New Year's Eve revels, then briefly recalled Avellino.

Leto said he accompanied Avellino to a series of taverns New Year's morning, from 1 until 5 a.m., then dropped him off about 5:30 a.m. at the Windsor Hotel, at the corner of Chippewa and Franklin streets.

Avellino said he registered at the hotel, but only stayed about 15 minutes because "the room was dirty" and strewn with beer bottles. He said he then left the hotel and strolled several blocks with an unnamed woman to Maryland and Seventh streets, where he said he witnessed the shooting. He said he then went back to the hotel because "I had to think." He said this time he stayed at the hotel about 45 minutes.

District Attorney Ball said he had learned this information subsequently to Avellino's previous testimony. Ball told the court Avellino "has since found he was registered at the Windsor Hotel early on the morning of January 1, 1960."

Asked by Condon why he had omitted mention of registering at the hotel in his original testimony, Avellino said, "I didn't think it was necessary, because I didn't sleep there."

Condon motioned that Avellino's entire testimony be stricken from the record on grounds that it was "so improbable, so contradictory, so unreasonable." Judge McCann denied the motion.

On Monday, July 18, the prosecution rested its case.

* *

THE PREVIOUS day—Sunday—the Rev. Dr. J. Palmer Muntz, the pastor of Cazenovia Park Baptist Church in Buffalo, preached a sermon the *Courier* reported on under the headline: "Pastor Queries Kennedy Loyalty."

> "If John Kennedy believes what he says he believes about the separation of church and state, he is not a good Catholic.

87

"In his denial of the authority of the Roman Catholic Church over him, he makes himself subject to excommunication. In fact, he ought to be excommunicated. But frankly, they won't do it."

Dr. Muntz referred to Kennedy's church-state declaration contained in his acceptance speech Friday at the Democratic National Convention in Los Angeles.

Accepting his nomination as the Democratic candidate for president, Sen. Kennedy had said: "I am telling you now what you are entitled to know: That my decision on every public policy will be my own—as an American, a Democrat, and a free man."

Dr. Muntz suggested the candidate may have had "mental reservations" concerning his declaration on his independence of action.

"I am not saying he did have mental reservations," Dr. Muntz remarked, but added that such mental reservations are approved by the Catholic Church when members are making public pronouncements…"

The pastor said, "we are opposing" Sen. Kennedy on the same grounds a Communist would be objected to. "Not because we don't like the man," he said, "but because of the philosophy and machinery of the group he represents."

Dr. Muntz intoned a selection of Catholic encyclicals and Catholic writers in declaring Sen. Kennedy would be under the control of the Roman Catholic Church. "The camel's nose is trying to get in the tent." Dr. Muntz said, "and our door is being closed now. Our liberty is threatened if Romanism gets a grip on the White House."

16.

WHEN THE defense took over is when things started getting interesting. But not right away.

Two witnesses were called who said they saw Catalano at locations several blocks from the church about the time he was alleged to have killed Father Belle. Louis Amoia said when he went to his father's house at 568 Busti Avenue about 7:20 a.m. to help his father start his truck, which wouldn't start because of the cold weather, he saw Catalano in front of his—Catalano's—house, 549 Busti, about four blocks from the murder location. Amoia described himself as a lifelong acquaintance of Catalano.

Amoia said he then went to the Peace Bridge Texaco station at Porter Avenue and Seventh Street for assistance—apparently they needed a jump start—and Stanley Tetro, an employee at the gas station, accompanied him back to 568 Busti in the service station Jeep. Tetro said that around 7:40 a.m. he saw Catalano at the corner of

Busti and Porter Avenue, about five blocks from the murder location. Tetro said he had never met Catalano, but "I saw him on the corner, and then the pictures in the paper."

MRS. MARY J. Vaccaro, who worked with Mrs. Congilosi in the Holy Cross School cafeteria, then testified that on the day of Father Belle's funeral, Mrs. Congilosi had told her: "Now my husband won't be accusing me of cheating anymore." Also about Mrs. Congilosi's domestic situation with regard to her husband. She said Mrs. Congilosi "rattled on practically every day about it." She added that she recalled no mention of Catalano in her conversations with Mrs. Congilosi. According to the *News* account:

> In October, Mrs. Vaccaro recalled, Mrs. Congilosi told her that "her husband was mistreating her."
>
> "She said he wouldn't even stay up in the house with them. She said there was a shed downstairs in the basement and he was sleeping there and cooking his meals there."
>
> Mrs. Vaccaro's testimony was introduced by Mr. Condon to counter testimony given by Mrs. Congilosi when he cross-examined her.
>
> At that time, Mrs. Congilosi answered "No" when Mr. Condon asked of her husband:
>
> "Does he live in the cellar?" and "Does he cook his meals in the cellar?"
>
> Mrs. Congilosi said then:

"He has a bedroom upstairs, next to the kitchen."

MRS. MAE Corliss, a clinic executive in the Buffalo General Hospital Outpatient Department, elaborated regarding the Congilosi domestic situation, based on what she said she had overheard Mrs. Congilosi telling other patients at the hospital, July 21, 1959. In the *News* account:

> "Mrs. Congilosi was talking about her husband," Mrs. Corliss said. "She said he had threatened to kill the whole family.
>
> "She said he had barricaded himself in the basement and they were terrified of him. She said he did not take his meals with the family and that he had a shotgun in the cellar and I think the words she used were a ground axe."

NEWS STORIES on the trial were typically without a by-line. *Courier* stories, on the other hand, often included a by-line. Up to this point, the *Courier* stories with a by-line were by Earl Williams. The *News* stories in general and Earl Williams's *Courier* stories seem fairly straightforward, objective accounts of the trial events. What was said and what was done. A bit colorless.

But now another reporter, Carol Johnson, takes over for the *Courier*. Her stories are typically more elaborate than the previous stories, featuring more dialogue and more description, and more of an effort to explain and interpret trial events.

Here is Carol Johnson's account of the testimony of Mrs. Corliss and several subsequent witnesses:

> Under the unwavering eyes of the all-male jury, Mrs. Corliss told of overhearing a conversation between Mrs. Congilosi and other women patients at the clinic July 21, 1959.
>
> Mrs. Corliss quoted Mrs. Congilosi as saying her husband had threatened to kill the whole family because of her "behavior." When Condon pressed her for an explanation of what was meant by "behavior," Mrs. Corliss replied:
>
> "Her husband accused her of having affairs with physicians at the hospital and even a priest."
>
> It became immediately apparent that Condon was attempting to shatter the prosecution's theory by showing Mrs. Congilosi's husband also had a motive for shooting the priest.
>
> He called Dr. Fraser L. Mooney, director of the hospital, and two nurses, Marion J. Bowman and Mrs. Neva M. Yager, head nurse in the outpatient department, to the witness stand. Condon was able to secure from Dr. Mooney confirmation that Mrs. Congilosi had been at the hospital on certain dates.
>
> When the defense attorney attempted to

question Dr. Mooney about the treatment given Mrs. Congilosi, however, the district attorney objected on grounds such information could not be given under doctor-patient privilege.

Ball made the same objection when Condon tried to question the nurses about conversations they had with Mrs. Congilosi. The inference was clear that he hoped to draw testimony from them similar to that of Mrs. Corliss.

When he asked Miss Bowman about a conversation with Mrs. Congilosi about "her problems," Ball immediately objected and was sustained by Visiting Judge Maurice McCann.

THE NEXT witness was Mrs. Ethel R. Brady, a psychiatric social worker at the hospital. According to the *Courier* story, Condon again tried to elicit testimony as to Mrs. Congilosi's medical problems and treatment. Again the prosecution objected on grounds of doctor-patient privilege.

Condon argued that the doctor-patient privilege did not extend to social workers. Ball argued—according to the *News* story—that it applied to any "agent" of the physician, or else the doctor-patient confidentiality guarantee would be meaningless.

Judge McCann called a recess to consider the matter. Following the recess, he ruled for the prosecution, against the defense.

According to the *Courier*, "Mrs. Brady was allowed to testify only on material which had no connection with Mrs. Congilosi's treatment at the hospital." Mrs. Brady's testimony then focused on a conversation between herself and Mrs. Congilosi in late January 1960, some weeks after the murder of Father Belle. The relevant portion of the *Courier* story is as follows:

> Mrs. Brady testified that she asked Mrs. Congilosi:
>
> "Was the priest your husband accused you of being unfaithful with Father Belle?"
>
> She said Mrs. Congilosi replied "Yes, he was."
>
> When asked by District Attorney Ball if Mrs. Congilosi referred to the defendant, Catalano, during the conversation, Mrs. Brady said:
>
> "She said her husband had protected her from Alfonso Catalano's accusations of infidelity with Father Belle."
>
> Ball asked if Mrs. Congilosi had named Catalano as her husband's source of information on her alleged infidelity with the priest. Mrs. Brady said she did not.

*   *

WHEN REPORTER Carol Johnson says, "it became immediately apparent that Condon was attempting to shatter the prosecution's theory [of the case] by showing Mrs. Congilosi's husband also had a motive for shooting the priest," that seems accurate. As for her further point that when Condon tried unsuccessfully to elicit information from the doctor and several nurses concerning Mrs. Congilosi's treatment under their care, "the inference was clear that he hoped to draw testimony from them similar to that of Mrs. Corliss," not so much. What he got from Mrs. Corliss—and the previous witness, Mrs. Vaccaro—was information about Mrs. Congilosi's problematical domestic situation, related to Mr. Congilosi's general hostility and anti-social character. That he did not take his meals with the family, but lived in the cellar, where he kept a shotgun and an ax. And threatened to kill her and the whole family because of what he seemed to believe—or maybe half-believed—about her having affairs with Father Belle and others. She must have been terrified of him. The whole family must have been terrified of him. But likely what Condon was trying but was unable to elicit from the medical personnel—as also from Mrs. Brady, the social worker—was information about Mrs. Congilosi's problems for which she was being treated at the hospital, which were possibly injuries incurred from physical abuse by Mr. Congilosi. We know that on the occasion when Father Belle intervened in the Congilosi domestic squabble, Mr. Congilosi had struck her.

17.

TO REBUT earlier testimony about a gun or guns supposedly in Catalano's possession, Joseph A. Marino, Catalano's son-in-law, who had sat with the defendant throughout the trial and translated trial events and statements to
him, testified that he had never seen his father-in-law with
a pistol.

In a slightly incongruous and somewhat pathetic note
that seemed to reveal a good deal about the defendant,
Marino was asked if he was "close" to his father-in-law. He
answered, "I tried to be a good son-in-law. But he's more
to himself."

THE DEFENSE rested its case. Whereupon, District Attorney Ball called two witnesses to refute a statement by
Phyllis Congilosi, the daughter of Mrs. Congilosi, that
seemed to contradict a subsequent statement by Mrs.
Congilosi. Neither of the papers had noted Phyllis Congilosi's statement at the time. The *Courier* account of the
rebuttal testimony was as follows:

> Ball also called two employees of Emergen-
> cy Hospital to testify in support of a statement
> made by Mrs. Mary Congilosi. During August
> and September of 1959, Mrs. Congilosi was em-

ployed at Emergency Hospital in the kitchen.

Mrs. Ann Hawkins, 210 Gray St., another worker, testified Mrs. Congilosi suffered a fall during work. Margaret M. Wagner, dietitian at the hospital, said she drove Mrs. Congilosi to Buffalo General Hospital after the fall at Mrs. Congilosi's request.

In earlier testimony, Phyllis Congilosi had testified her mother fell at home, although Mrs. Congilosi maintained she had fallen only at work.

18.

THE DEFENSE summation featured a free-wheeling attack on Avellino as a credible witness, credible person. From the *News* report:

> "Rudy is a misfit in society…He swore one thing and then another. This man never worked more than two weeks in the last year. He's a man who can't remember where he sleeps."

And on procedural matters related to the same witness:

> Mr. Condon charged that Avellino had not been confronted by a lineup when he identified

Catalano as the man he saw coming from the church garage.

"There is a way to get a bona fide showup," said Mr. Condon. "It is not by putting a white man with a black man or a six-footer with a midget, but by putting men together of similar build.

"In this case, they took Rudy to the office and said, 'Is he the man?' And Rudy says, 'Yes.'"

The defense summation lasted two and a half hours. Condon went over the trial exhibit-by-exhibit and witness-by-witness, pointing out what he considered to be contradictions and inconsistencies in the prosecution case, plus failures by the police to fully investigate the case.

He described the case against Catalano as "a horrible web of circumstances," and "only circumstantial evidence without Avellino's eye-witness report." From the *Courier* report:

> The defense attorney also said that Catalano was "a sitting duck" for Mary Congilosi to deflect her husband's suspicions.
>
> Condon further intimated that police had not done further checking once Catalano was arrested.
>
> "This was going down one street just like an express train," he said.

THE PROSECUTION summation was pretty straight-forward apparently, summed up in a few sentences in the papers.

In the *Courier* report, Ball said Catalano was a lonely man who was interested in Mary Congilosi "as a house-keeper." He said Catalano caused doubts in Mr. Congilosi's mind concerning Mrs. Congilosi's fidelity, and then shot Father Belle because the priest was interfering in Catalano's own plans with regard to Mrs. Congilosi. Ball accused the defense of trying to draw a picture of "a giant conspiracy."

The *News* gave no further details.

*　　*

"'A SITTING duck' for Mary Congilosi to deflect her husband's suspicions." Subjective or objective genitive, Stephen Dedalus might ask. Suspicions of—that is, by—Mr. Congilosi, about her possible romantic involvement with Father Belle and others? Or more likely objective genitive. Suspicions of—that is, about—Mr. Congilosi, as the actual killer. Surely that was the idea Condon wanted the jury to consider. The alternative theory of the case that he was never able to propound openly. And—also to consider—that the police never fully investigated. But only investigated Catalano, as a sitting duck. (Or in an alternative animal metaphor, a scapegoat.)

19.

IN HIS charge to the jury, Judge McCann listed four possible verdicts: first-degree murder, second-degree murder, first-degree-manslaughter, or acquittal. He explained that the elements of first-degree murder included "not only an intent to kill, but also a deliberate and premeditated design to kill…such deliberate and premeditated design must precede the killing by some space of time." Whereas, second-degree murder "implies intent to kill, but no premeditation." And first-degree manslaughter would be "killing without a design to effect death, in heat of passion or by means of a dangerous weapon."

THE CASE went to the jury Wednesday, July 20, about 5:30 p.m., and deliberations continued until about 1:30 a.m, after which the jury was sequestered for the rest of the night in the Statler Hotel. The jury had returned to the courtroom once that evening to re-hear testimony by two people who said they saw Catalano at the 7 a.m. Mass at Holy Cross Church on New Year's day, and by Avellino, the eye-witness.

ON THURSDAY the jury deliberated all day, breaking just for lunch and dinner, and returning twice to the courtroom to re-hear testimony.

The jury requested re-reading of—or of parts of—the

direct and cross-examination testimony of Mrs. Congilo-si, her daughter Phyllis, her sister Mrs. Swier, and Homicide Detective Sergeant Joseph T. McCarthy. (McCarthy was briefly mentioned in newspaper accounts in January as an investigator in the case, but neither paper had previously noted he had testified at the trial, nor was the nature of his testimony described.)

After the jurors left the courtroom, Condon objected that they had not heard an adequate portion of the cross-examination testimony. Whereupon, over an objection by the prosecution, the judge recalled the jurors and had them hear further cross-examination material.

The testimony that was then re-read included Mrs. Congilosi's affirmative reply when asked whether, prior to the New Year's day street encounter with Catalano, her husband had been taken to police headquarters for questioning about the murder.

*　*

NEITHER OF the papers had previously noted that it had ever been mentioned in testimony that Mr. Congilosi had been a suspect.

(Possibly reflecting an overzealous journalistic disposition toward the prosecution side of the proceedings. A point Condon would make in an interview years later.)

In fact, Mr. Congilosi was the initial suspect, as noted in a *News* story in January. Though totally as if in passing, ("Ironically, the woman's husband was first considered a possible suspect in Father Belle's murder.")

20.

JURY DELIBERATIONS continued into Friday. The jury asked to re-hear testimony by Father Caligiuri, who had discovered the body, and Timothy McLaren, the fiancé of Phyllis Congilosi, as well as the part of Judge McCann's charge to the jury relating to direct and circumstantial evidence.

When the jury returned to deliberations, Condon again objected to what had been read and not read. The judge overruled the objection. The *News* explained the rather complicated business as follows:

> The attorney contended that some sections were read and others were not. He also maintained that the jury should not have heard the section on "admissions" made by the defendant, in preference to other portions of the charge.
>
> "Just a minute, we were just complying with the jury's request," declared Judge McCann.
>
> "They didn't request the section on admissions," persisted Mr. Condon. "I suggest other sections more pertinent might have been read."
>
> "I suggest," Judge McCann advised, "that you put it on the record."
>
> Mr. Condon then proceeded to cite for the court stenographer the sections he had chosen.

THE *NEWS* account said the "admissions" related to a statement Detective Vingoe said Catalano made the night of January 2 in police headquarters: "I wish the good Lord would strike me dead for the awful thing I have done."

The defense had contended that that statement was made involuntarily, after the defendant had been questioned for some time.

ON FRIDAY afternoon Condon asked the judge to declare a mistrial. He said the jury had been deliberating for so long by then that "a verdict now could only come through coercion. It would only mean a matter of persuasion one way or the other."

The judge denied the request. "The jury has not indicated it cannot come to a verdict," he stated, "and I refuse to interfere until such time as they so inform me."

THE VERDICT was announced late Friday evening. Not guilty. To an outburst of cheers and shouts of joy from the packed courtroom. Judge McCann rapped for order.

The decision was relayed to Catalano by his son-in-law, Joseph Marino, who had been acting as interpreter for his father-in-law.

Marino said later that Catalano had not understood the foreman's announcement. When Catalano was told the decision, he smiled, but then resumed the stoical attitude he had maintained throughout the trial.

Released from custody, he walked slowly to the hall outside the courtroom, where he was hugged and congratulated by relatives and friends.

A front-page picture in the *Courier* shows Catalano—looking a little dazed by his ordeal—being embraced by two daughters, Mrs. Joseph Marino, of Hamburg, and Mrs. Salvatore LoTempio, from San Jose, California.

An inside-page picture showed him giving his attorney, John Condon, a kiss on the cheek.

JURY FOREMAN Lloyd R. Garrison was reluctant to discuss the deliberations with the papers, but indicated the key question for the jury was "the credibility and validity of the testimony of one witness."

He declined to reveal which witness that was, but both papers were confident it was Avellino, the supposed eye-witness, who "admitted on the witness stand that he had lied in certain statements he made before the grand jury which indicted Catalano," according to the *Courier*.

> Garrison added voluntarily, however, that of the several juries on which he has served:
>
> "This jury was unquestionably the most conscientious. They were perfect. Their approach was more systematic and factual than any jury I've ever been on."
>
> Asked whether the question of religion had arisen during the deliberations, he replied, emphatically:
>
> "Absolutely not."

FOLLOWING THE verdict, the *Courier* reported, Joseph Marino, the son-in-law,

> ...sought out several of the jurors, clasped their hands warmly and said in a broken voice: "Thank you so much."
>
> He told reporters, however, that Catalano understood "very little" of what transpired during the trial.
>
> "I didn't tell him everything," Marino explained. "I had to keep his spirits up. When he would hear his name mentioned, he would ask me, 'What are they saying about me?'
>
> "I told him, 'It's okay, Papa. It's not too bad.'"

Catalano showed little or no emotion following the verdict, but seemed tired. Asked whether he was going to celebrate his acquittal, he said, "No, no. I'm going to sleep."

Mrs. LoTempio said she and her husband planned to take her father back to California to live with them.

21.

A BRIEF story in the *Courier* several days later said that Avellino was awarded $129 in witness fees in connection with the trial, at a rate of $3 per day, for 43 days. During that entire time, the story said, Avellino had been in jail, serving sentences for third-degree assault, and for contempt of court in connection with a civil case.

The paper said that "it may have been Avellino's testimony which swung the jury to vote acquittal" in the case.

A NOTICE on Avellino in the *News* the same day did not mention the witness fees, but said that Avellino, 33 years old, was to be sentenced the next day for stealing from the mails, a sentence that had been pending since January.

The notice said Avellino had been charged the previous September with forging and cashing a $54 income tax refund check, on which charge he was subsequently convicted, and had been released on his own recognizance awaiting sentencing, but then was locked up as a material witness in the Belle case.

22.

IT DIDN'T make sense. It never made sense.

Catalano, an old widower, romantically pursues Mrs. Amato, the widow of his recently deceased lifelong best friend, and when she rejects him, pursues her daughter, Mrs. Congilosi, a married woman with eight children. But at the same time accuses Mrs. Congilosi to her husband of having affairs with several men, including a local parish priest, Father Belle.

But also accuses the husband of unspecified wrongdoing, and threatens to kill him. And also accuses Father Belle—via a crudely lettered sign posted in the back of the parish church and a telephone call to the pastor—of unspecified wrongdoing. Something to do with a lover. And murders Father Belle, for supposedly interfering in his—Catalano's—supposed pursuit of Mrs. Congilosi. Perhaps by way of his—Belle's—own romantic involvement with Mrs. Congilosi.

Meanwhile, everyone from the mayor to the bishop to the pastor to the chief of police in charge of the investigation to an array of parishoners attests to the saintliness of the slain priest. And any allegations against him—but these are all from Catalano—are dismissed as mere slander. A product of the imagination of a madman. In accord with the official theory of the case—literally from day one, based on the saintliness premise—that the crime had to have been the work of a madman. And so Catalano is charged.

Later information—trial testimony—indicates some of the husband's wrongdoings. He is said to have been wildly jealous regarding his wife's alleged extramarital activities, and threatened to kill her and several or perhaps all of their eight children into the bargain. A man of violent propensities, it seems, who on one occasion at least struck Mrs. Congilosi, an occasion when Father Belle was present, and called the police, who took Mr. Congilosi in for questioning.

Mr. Congilosi was initially considered a suspect in the murder of Father Belle—he was the initial suspect—and was questioned again at that time by the police, but not charged, and we hear no more about him until his name comes up—but almost as if incidentally—at the trial. But we don't see or hear from him at the trial. He is not called as a witness.

In addition, a supposed eye-witness to the murder said he heard shots and saw Catalano run from the garage where Father Belle was later found dead in his car. A linchpin witness in the case against Catalano, seemingly. But whose testimony is so unconvincing—he is himself so unconvincing as a credible witness, as a credible person—he ultimately seems to be the reason—more than anyone or anything else—for the not guilty verdict.

*   *

I STRUGGLED with this material for years. Wanting to write about it, but not writing, basically because I couldn't understand it.

Working on it for a while, then putting it down, frustrated. Alternating regular periods of renewed energy and enthusiasm and determination to get to the bottom of the matter, and longer periods of virtual abandonment of the project, in discouragement and dismay at the muddled amalgam of dubious truths and outright lies and anomalies and contradictions. The story that didn't make sense.

Then picking it up again. Going back to the records, the papers, on downtown public library microfilm, smudged and scratched and sullied after years of handling and mishandling by local history buffs and genealogists and general nostalgists.

Initially, taking notes in longhand on yellow legal pads. Then photocopying key portions of newspaper articles. Then back again for further portions, until ultimately having photocopied a virtual complete set of all relevant articles, from both papers, for the week or so following the murder, then the month-long period of the trial.

But always after a few weeks of re-reading and pondering, giving it up again. Still in the dark. More baffled and frustrated than ever.

Until, in a last-ditch attempt to fathom the refractory material, launching on a painstaking thorough collation of the two papers' reports, to try to create as complete as possible an overall account of the murder and trial events, incorporating all anomalies and contradictions. All manner of weirdness. A result of which was that the anomalies and contradictions appeared to be authentic component parts of the story, rather than as I had previously considered phantom effects of my own simple inability to understand. From my own lack of staying power, or eye power, or brain power.

BUT THEN who did kill Father Belle? If Catalano didn't.

That is, the official version now was that Catalano—having been duly acquitted by a jury—didn't do it. Versus the nonetheless robust unofficial version—of the police and prosecutors—that he did. Just that he got lucky. Got a good lawyer, and a good jury, and got off. Allowing the police and prosecutors to wash their hands of the matter. Walk away from an unsolved murder. There was no further investigation.

I thought Catalano in fact didn't do it. Not because he was acquitted (which could as easily have gone the other way). But just because it didn't make sense.

23.

WHAT INITIALLY drew me to the story was the altarpiece. The aesthetic object. Beautiful with a kind of terrible beauty. About transforming swords into plowshares. Instruments of violence into an ancillary item to the Church principal liturgical act of reconciliation. In the wake of the Father Belle murder. Even possibly incorporating the actual instruments of violence—component portions of the actual instruments—of the Father Belle murder. Transformed and untransformed. (Thus possibly also containing a clue or clues to solving the unsolved crime.)

It had to be—somehow, I thought—that among the myriad shells were the shells of the actual bullets that killed the priest. Concealed and unconcealed. Via a possible scenario such as I imagined likely also accounted for the collage artwork I had seen in the rectory, by the same artist-priest. Who on a temporary summer priestly assignment to the parish, would have been provided a room with maybe just a bed and dresser and desk as furniture. And in stowing his shirts and socks and underwear in the dresser drawers, and other items in desk drawers, discovers some odds and ends items left by a previous occupant. An old theater or concert ticket stub, a dilapidated old black and white photo. Stuff someone once had saved as memorabilia, but then in packing to move out, wittingly or unwittingly left behind. Items with no meaning to the artist-priest except that they seemed to have been someone's memorabilia. Whereupon the artist-priest conceived to make a collage artwork of them. About the idea of memorabilia. Memorabilia in the abstract.

And for the altarpiece—a possible scenario—that in one of the dresser or desk drawers, the artist-priest finds one or more bullet shells. No idea what or where they are from. Why they are there. But knowing something—not even that much, perhaps—about the Father Belle murder, begins to wonder, could there be a connection somehow. And begins to think, yes, possibly so. That the shells might be—somehow—from the bullets that killed Father Belle.

In which case—why the shells would have been in a drawer in the rectory, and not have been turned over to the police or other authorities, as ordinary and proper in the case of evidentiary materials—suggesting something amiss. Something to hide. Something more to hide. Some involvement. An inside job.

And a further possible scenario for how they got into a drawer in the rectory in the first place—if one of the parish priests first persons on scene—maybe even Msgr. Gambino—but there was no report that Msgr. Gambino visited the garage in the wake of the incident—but one or other of the assistants who did visit the garage—before or even after the arrival of medical personnel and the police—for it was not a crime scene initially, there were no apparent signs of foul play, but Father Belle was thought to have died of natural causes—discovers some spent shells on the garage floor, and unobtrusively retrieves them and pockets them, and then later sequesters them in a drawer somewhere in the rectory. Or possibly hands them over to Msgr. Gambino—for safekeeping, or to decide what to do with them—who sequesters them.

BUT WHICH of the priests? Who would have had a motive in the crime? Not likely any of Father Belle's fellow assistants at the parish. There seemed no reason to doubt the general sentiment that Belle was well-liked. It was far-fetched to think one of his fellow assistants might have murdered him. Though Msgr. Gambino perhaps. Who was told Father Belle was doing something improper. Never clearly specified what. Msgr. Gambino denied the allegations were true. But if the allegations were true—if Father Belle was involved in some impropriety—Msgr. Gambino would have been most sensible of the potential scandal to the Catholic Church in general and Holy Cross Church in particular, the parish, the community. The parish Msgr. Gambino had founded and that was his great life's work. The community he had watched grow and prosper—and Msgr. Gambino had been a principal guide and director of that growth—from a poor and despised immigrant group to a respected key component of the larger social, economic, and political community.

If Father Belle was in fact involved in some impropriety, Msgr. Gambino would have considered long and hard how to put a stop to it. And no doubt tried to do so—by means of his substantial powers both of moral suasion and ecclesiastical authority—talking to Father Belle, counseling him, even threatening him with some sort of Church law comeuppance—but failed. And having failed, decided the best recourse—only recourse—was the rather more radical one of eliminating Father Belle. Killing him.

Msgr. Gambino's venerable status and position in the Church and the community would assure that he would not be suspected. Would not even be questioned. He never was seriously questioned, apparently, in the days and weeks after the murder, or at the trial.

I DIDN'T think it likely that Msgr. Gambino would have pulled the trigger. But someone could have done that for him. He could have hired someone. There was the Mafia, after all. Then he could have visited the scene, either before or after the discovery of the body by the assistant, and casually picked up the shells (you hire help these days and then you have to clean up after them) before anyone else had seen them (mostly because no one else would have been looking), and stuck them in a pocket, then later sequestered them in a desk or dresser drawer in the rectory. Scarcely concealed. But there was no chance they would be discovered by the authorities. There would be no search in the rectory.

Or again—since there was no indication in any of the newspaper reports that Msgr. Gambino had visited the garage in the wake of the discovery of the incident—if one of the assistants picked up a shell or shells from the garage floor, very possibly he would have turned them over to Gambino. And Gambino then would have put them in a drawer somewhere. Where they remained sequestered for the rest of his life. And after his death. Until the artist-priest happened upon them. And conceived to make the altarpiece.

I CALLED this the Gambino scenario. It included Msgr. Gambino's desperate solution to a moral dilemma—to take drastic measures to put a stop to an impropriety and avert a ruinous scandal—and then—to conceal the drastic measures crime and avert an additional ruinous scandal—to sequester evidentiary materials. And the artist-priest's corollary dilemma—to continue the concealment of evidentiary materials—if that's what the shells were—and chain of crimes—or end the sequester and chain by exposing the evidentiary materials to public notice—but nonetheless entailing scandal—that he solved in a brilliant artistic act and object that reveals but yet conceals.

*   *

BASED ON ballistics tests, it was determined that the gun was a revolver, in which case no shells would have been ejected, and no shells retrieved from the garage floor. Pretty much demolishing the Gambino scenario. At least as imagined. Fancied. Fantasized.

Still, I thought, there had to be some connection between the bullet shells altarpiece and the murder of a priest of the parish. Possibly somehow including actual incident shells in the altarpiece.

It kept me going back. Re-reading the newspaper accounts. Thinking about the anomalies and contradictions. Talking to friends—anyone who would listen, really—about the case. Trying to make sense of it.

(Nor did I rule out that Msgr. Gambino—who had a motive for getting rid of Father Belle—and a kind of venerability immunity—could have had some connection with the murder.)

*   *

MUCH LATER—years later—when the altarpiece was located at St. Joseph's, and occasionally on display in the rear of the sanctuary, I got permission from one of the parish officials to come in sometime when the church was empty and examine the piece closely and carefully. To see if I could discover, concealed as it were among the multitude of shells, one or several somehow different from the rest. So possibly from the bullets that killed Father Belle. In my cursory first look at the piece, at Holy Cross, during my impromptu tour of the church with Dan Walsh, the shells seemed to be entirely .22-caliber, the only type of ammunition and gun—other than a shotgun—I had any actual experience with, from owning and often firing a .22-caliber rifle during my years on the farm. Whereas, it was established that the murder bullets were .32-caliber, which I assumed would be noticeably a bit larger than .22-caliber.

But not being particularly knowledgeable in general about firearms, I asked a friend along on the St. Joseph's excursion who would have been, Michael O'Rourke, a lawyer and former state trooper. But our close and careful examination of the altarpiece revealed nothing. The shells in the altarpiece seemed to be all the same. Entirely .22-caliber. No shells from the bullets that killed Father Belle.

24.

I TESTED the Gambino scenario on Dan Walsh. He said he didn't think it was possible. Not on some pietistical basis that a priest or worse a monsignor, and of such eminence, could not commit a murder, but just that it was contrary to what he thought he knew—had heard—of Msgr. Gambino.

He told me a story he had heard. A true story, he assured me. A known Mafia figure in the community had died, and it was supposed and expected by the family that he would be buried from Holy Cross Church. That is, with a requiem Mass and all traditional Church funeral rites. But then the morning of the funeral, when the hearse and other vehicles arrived at Holy Cross, the church building was dark. The lights were off. But Msgr. Gambino could be clearly seen standing in the church doorway, arms folded across his chest in an unmistakable attitude of defiance.

After some minutes of silent standoff—hearse and cortege in the street, priest in the doorway, nobody moving, nobody emerging from any of the vehicles—the hearse and cortege move on. Straight on to the cemetery apparently. No final Church blessing for this guy. Not from Holy Cross at least.

I SAID I thought it was possible Father Belle was involved with a woman. Dan allowed it was possible, but didn't think so. He suggested maybe what I should be looking at was a homosexual connection. I asked him if he knew anything in that regard about Father Belle. He said he didn't know anything specifically, but said he thought in general in a case involving clergy, homosexuality had to be considered.

He mentioned the Msgr. O'Connor murder. I vaguely remembered that one. The body was found floating in Scajaquada Creek, near Delaware Park. Dan said he had heard that that had been a homosexual matter.

This was the 'seventies or 'eighties. When many or most Catholics would have been appalled at the suggestion of a Catholic priest being a homosexual. (Homosexual acts were condemned by the Church as sinful as an aberration of the natural order, in addition to being illegal in New York State until 1980, and in the United States overall until 2003. And subject throughout those years and decades to a level of general opprobrium that by now thankfully has much abated, if certainly not entirely disappeared.) I was shocked when in our discussion Dan talked matter-of-factly about the prevalence of homosexuality among the clergy. (In my naïveté.) He didn't put a percentage number on it, but indicated just that it was not at all unknown.

*　*

THE NAME struck a bell. Msgr. O'Connor. At first I couldn't place it. Then it hit me. One of the acolytes in the picture taken at Father Belle's first Mass. Father Belle's good friend—best friend—from the seminary.

I looked up the O'Connor murder, in the Monday, March 13, 1966, *Courier-Express*. In addition to the main story on O'Connor, the paper ran a front-page sidebar on Father Belle, on the irony of the two murdered priests having been good friends. The story noted that Father Belle had assisted at Msgr. O'Connor's first Mass, as subdeacon.

At the time of his death, O'Connor was the editor of the diocesan newspaper. His body had been found Sunday afternoon by three boys walking alongside the creek. It was estimated O'Connor had died late Saturday night or possibly early Sunday morning. It was initially thought his death was due to natural causes, and an autopsy was scheduled for Monday morning. It was speculated he might have suffered a dizzy spell while walking along the creek bank and fallen into the water and drowned. The paper said Msgr. O'Connor had been ill of late. But when his car could not be located, and his wallet was not found in his clothing, foul play was suspected, and the autopsy was moved up and was begun late Sunday night.

The autopsy revealed death by drowning, and what were initially considered "superficial" body bruises that could have been suffered in a fall. But when it was discovered the injuries included a small broken bone in the neck, the case was declared a homicide.

Moreover, in addition to the missing wallet, it was revealed the victim's shoes were missing. These were discovered on the other side of the creek from where the body was found. His car was found near the corner of Lincoln Parkway and Chatham Avenue, some blocks away from where the body was found, and was said to have blood stains on the upholstery, and bits of soil that were said to have come from the shoulders of the Scajaquada Expressway. (How this was determined was not explained. The expressway is a four-lane, limited-access highway cutting roughly east-west across the northern part of the city's west side. There is little noticeable soil on the shoulders of the Scajaquada Expressway.)

But then after a week or so, the story dropped from the newspapers. The police investigation—with no suspects identified, apparently, and no real leads, as far as one could tell from the papers—was dropped or shelved. There was nothing in the papers about any possible homosexual angle.

DAN WALSH told another story. He said some years previously he had met and talked with some high official in the Buffalo Police homicide division. He didn't name the official. On some vague pastoral mission, I got the impression. Vague possibly even to Dan, it seemed. Someone had suggested he meet and talk with this man, who may have been going through some sort of personal or spiritual crisis. So Dan went to see him, in the official's office. And they talked about whatever it was they talked about. And toward the end of the visit, as Dan was about to leave, the official pointed to a file lying on his desk and told Dan—off-handedly as it were, with no connection whatever to whatever else they had talked about—it was the Msgr. O'Connor file—only pertinent information in that Dan was a Catholic priest, and so would probably be interested in a case about another priest—and that it would be going home with him—the official—that evening, and straight into his fireplace.

SOME TIME later, talking to another priest, I asked him if to his knowledge the Msgr. O'Connor murder was a homosexual matter. I told him of my interest in the Father Belle murder, and that I was interested in the O'Connor murder—particularly given that they were friends—as possibly related. I said I thought there was more to the Father Belle matter than the police and prosecutors made out. That perhaps Belle wasn't the saintly innocent they pretended. I suggested—as an aside—that if the O'Connor murder happened at the present time—whenever that was, I can't remember, years ago, but years after the incident—and it was a homosexual matter, the police and civil officials would not conceal that aspect. (I may have been over-confident on that score.)

He agreed. And said there were rumors that the O'Connor murder was a homosexual matter, but he didn't know for certain.

But he mentioned that he had heard a story about a police official—seemingly some other official than the man in the Dan Walsh story—who told a priest—seemingly some other priest than Dan Walsh, though possibly this was the same story transmuted through multiple oral transmissions—regarding the O'Connor investigation, that the police file on the investigation was now "at the bottom of the river."

*   *

A HALF a century and more after the Msgr. O'Connor murder, the *Buffalo News* revisited the story. November 13, 2018. So not a particular anniversary of the event, the usual pretext for newspaper historical update stories. But the point of the update story seemed not so much historical remembrance as possible relation to breaking news over previous months about the astonishing number of Buffalo priests that had been credibly accused to diocesan authorities over past decades of child-abuse crimes, but the information was not made public by the diocese. Including not communicated to civil legal authorities, the police and district attorney. Often the miscreant priests were simply transferred to another parish in the diocese, or sometimes another parish in another diocese. (And in either case a new set of potential victims.)

The O'Connor update story, by reporter Dan Herbeck, was entitled: "Cold Case: Whispers of cover-up remain decades after priest's murder." The story told how after several weeks of intense police investigation of the O'Connor murder, the inquiry seemed suddenly and abruptly to have been shut down. With the clear suggestion—as the ultimate point of the story—that Church authorities had intervened.

Which may in the O'Connor case have had to do with another priest emerging as a suspect, or to a possible homosexual aspect of the crime. (The story did not directly allude to any homosexual aspect. But reading between the lines.)

The story also pointed out that O'Connor and Belle had once been "the best of friends," but also that "there has never been any suggestion by police that the two cases were connected."

ANOTHER DAN Herbeck story some months later, May 19/20, 2019, was entitled: "Marching orders kept Buffalo cops from arresting child-molesting priests." Marching orders again pretty clearly coming from the Catholic Church hierarchy. It quoted a retired police officer who had investigated vice crimes for almost twenty years saying, "The department's unwritten policy was that Catholic priests did not get arrested." Another former vice squad officer said, "When you picked up a priest, you had to call the bishop's office. The bishop's office would send someone to pick up the priest. No arrest was made."

A SIDEBAR story to the "marching orders" story outlined what happened in lieu of legal system arrest and prosecution of miscreant priests apprehended by police for whatever sort of illicit activity. There was a priest in Buffalo from the 1950s to the 1980s, Msgr. Franklin Kelliher, a former heavyweight champion boxer, who in addition to his priestly duties and activities, worked as a professional wrestler, known as "The Masked Marvel." The main reason for the mask was to hide his true identity. In those years, if a priest was caught by civil authorities in some kind of compromising activity or situation, he wasn't arrested and prosecuted, but instead handed over by the police to Msgr. Kelliher, who would simply physically beat the hell out of him. I heard that once—in the process—he killed a man. I don't know if that's true. But I think, not impossible.

25.

BACK NOW to around the late 1970s, I worked at a public housing organization with a guy—a friend—whose wife's maiden name was Catalano. I asked her once if she had ever heard of the Father Belle case, and if by chance she was related to Alfonso Catalano. I was surprised when she said yes on both counts. That she remembered the incident—since she would have been very young at the time, no more than about five or six years old, I guessed—and that Alfonso Catalano was her great-uncle. And further surprised at the sense of shame—mortification—she clearly felt about the matter. Again, particularly since she would have been so young at the time. She would have gotten her understanding and feelings about the matter via the no doubt voluble discussion and palpable emotions at the time of the grown-ups in the family.

She was reluctant to talk much about the matter. But insisted that Catalano was innocent. I told her I agreed. I said I thought he was innocent, too. She said the episode was extremely painful to the whole family. The terrible accusations, the humiliating publicity.

Later I talked with her older brother about the matter. Who seemed less sensitive about it than his sister. He confirmed that Alfonso Catalano was their great-uncle, and showed me family photos of Catalano as a much younger man. Maybe then in his thirties.

The brother told me that after the trial Alfonso Catalano left the area. He didn't know where he went, or anything more about it. But then, after a number of years, Catalano returned to Western New York. And on his first day back, he was struck by a car and killed.

THE BROTHER didn't know when that was. When Catalano died. I tried to find out. Social Security records indicated that the last Social Security check issued to Alfonso Catalano—at the Hamburg address of his daughter and the son-in-law who interpreted for him at the trial—was in December 1972. I searched the newspapers from around that time for a death notice or a news item about the accident, but didn't find anything.

I COULDN'T imagine it would have been just a coincidence, getting killed the first day back. I thought what would have happened was that whoever—whatever forces—had killed Father Belle—or knew who killed him—and then tried to have Catalano take the fall, might have told Catalano, after the trial, to leave town and not return. And he did leave. But then, years later, did return. And they killed him.

I DON'T know if that's what happened. But it might have been. Because it was hard to believe it would have been just a coincidence. Getting killed the first day back.

26.

I WROTE to John Condon, at his law firm, Condon and Traheri, in Williamsville, a Buffalo suburb. I said I was interested in the Father Belle case, that I was trying to write something about it, and would he be willing to talk to me about it. I asked if he could give me a call, and we could set up a meeting at his convenience. I thought we might have lunch.

He called six months later. He sounded skeptical. He wanted to know what I was up to, why I was interested in the case. He wanted to know about me. (I felt a little like I was on a witness stand, under cross-examination.)

I tried to talk fast (to not lose him). I said I became interested in the case when a priest friend showed me around Holy Cross Church, and there was a memorial plaque in the vestibule to Father Belle. I said I vaguely recalled the murder, which had happened when I was in college, but then I went and looked up the newspaper accounts. I said there were some aspects of the case that didn't make sense to me, and I wanted to ask him some questions. I said I thought he could help me.

He was hard of hearing. I had to speak up. I had to practically shout into the phone. And a couple of times repeat what I had just said.

He wanted to know where I had gone to school, to college. I said I went to Canisius College, then gone away to graduate school. (Canisius was the right answer. That's where he went, he told me later, though I might have guessed. About ten years before me.)

He still wanted to know why I was interested in the case.

I said I had read the newspaper accounts, several times over, and it still didn't completely make sense to me. I said I thought there was more to the case than met the eye.

"What are you saying," he blurted, "that my guy was guilty?"

I thought now I was going to lose him. He was going to hang up. "No, no," I responded. "I think your guy was innocent. I think he was set up. I think there was a cover-up."

There was dead silence. Immediately I regretted what I had said. I had way overstated. Those were big words. Set up. Cover-up. I couldn't prove those things. Now I would get it, I thought. Now he knows I don't know what I'm talking about. I prepared for the worst.

The silence continued. Forever. Ten seconds. Fifteen. It felt like fifteen minutes. Finally, he broke it. He said, slowly, deliberately: "You know, you may be on the right track." I almost fell over.

HE SAID it had been a long time. He didn't remember everything. I said I could probably fill him in on some of the details. I had read the newspaper accounts several times.

He said he remembered there was this priest, or monsignor—he couldn't remember his name at first—who was very prominent in the community.

"Msgr. Gambino," I prompted.

"Yes, Msgr. Gambino," he said. "He was, he was…" He searched for the word.

"Venerable," I offered.

"Yes, venerable," he said, seizing on it.

He said it was nothing you could put your finger on, but there was a subtle pressure not to question Msgr. Gambino at length, or too closely. To handle him with kid gloves. He said he was a young and fresh lawyer at the time, and "a good Catholic boy." And so, without thinking much about it, without really realizing it, was susceptible to the pressure. Moreover, he said, he had previously worked in the DA's office and was friendly with prosecuting attorney Ball (of whom he spoke highly) and other attorneys in that office, who he said would have been a prime source of the subtle pressure not to question Gambino.

HE KEPT having difficulty hearing me over the phone—he said it was because of his hearing loss that he had had to retire—so that I was uncomfortable trying to conduct what I hoped would be a lengthy interview over the phone. I suggested we meet and talk face to face.

"Sure," he said. "How often do you get down to Boca Raton?"

I said I thought he was in Williamsville. He said, no, he lived in Florida now. But he said he came back from time to time—he still had a home in Hamburg, a suburb south of Buffalo—and we could meet and talk the next time he was back. He said he was coming back in about two months, at Easter time. We agreed to get together then.

*   *

WE MET on a Saturday morning at his house in Hamburg. He was small of stature, but seemed full of energy, full of fight. Wizened-looking, gristly. An old prizefighter who remained lean and taut and in trim beyond his competitive years. He gave the impression throughout the interview of missing the old courtroom arena. The feel and smell of the canvas and leather, the sparring and jousting with witnesses, the brisk tattoo of sharp jabs that unsteadied an opponent at the knees, then getting him on the ropes, with trademark left hook, right cross combination, finishing him off. On the balls of his feet, bouncing back to a neutral corner. All in a day's work.

He wore a new-looking gray sweatshirt with a small red logo—La Nova—on the upper left breast. La Nova, a pizzeria in the heart of the West Side of Buffalo, is famous for excellent Italian food. There is a short list of about three or four pizzerias in Buffalo that aficionados—which would be most of the population of Western New York—could come to blows over arguments as to which is the very best. La Nova would be on that short list. In addition, La Nova was well-known for being the legitimate business of Joseph Todaro, a reputed—but not proven—Mafia figure.

He fed me coffee, and after another barrage of his questions about me—schools, jobs, personal life, again why I was interested in the Father Belle case—I elbowed in with some questions for him. I had written out in a notebook the questions I wanted to ask him, and took notes on his answers.

FOR STARTERS, he said, it was a long time ago, and many particulars he wouldn't be able to recall. But he could talk about his general impressions about the case, and some particulars were still vivid.

He said Alfonso Catalano was a terrible client. He was suspicious of everybody, including Condon. Wouldn't talk to him. He said Catalano was a bootlegger from prohibition days, and now—at the time of the murder—a sort of would-be underworld type, who projected a tough-guy swagger that was essentially bluff. Basically, he thought, Catalano wanted to be seen as somebody important and respected in the community. Which probably translated in his mind into feared and respected. But there wasn't much behind it.

Asked if he thought Catalano owned a gun, Condon said he didn't doubt he owned a gun, but doubted he had ever used a gun in his life.

By way of indicating that he knew whereof he spoke regarding demimonde, he pointed to the La Nova logo on his shirt, and mentioned Todaro's reputed Mafia connection. He said he was Todaro's personal attorney for many years, and noted that he had always been successful in extricating his client from whatever legal accusation or predicament.

He said Catalano had a car, which was a status symbol in the community, and frequently provided transportation for friends and acquaintances. It had been said that he drove Mrs. Congilosi and her son to the boy's special school out of the city, and drove Phyllis Congilosi to work, and Timothy McLaren to Canisius College. Partly as a way of enhancing his status among these people, surely, but partly also, it would seem, out of a basic good nature, goodness of heart. Condon said he believed Catalano had some property—or maybe just access to property—south of the city, along the lake—possibly this would have been the son-in-law's property on the lake—and part of his connection to the Congilosi family—in addition to having been a lifelong friend of Mrs. Congilosi's late father—was that from time to time he would drive some of the Congilosis for a day in the country, by the lake.

CONDON RECALLED an incident early on in the proceedings. He said prosecution and defense attorneys had agreed among themselves to postpone the trial until the early fall. Basically to give everyone a chance to have a summer vacation. That agreement had to be approved by the judge, however, after a hearing, at which the defendant had to be present and give his assent. Assent and approval should have been pro forma. However, at the hearing, when Catalano understood what was being proposed, he would not agree, but said he needed the trial to get underway as soon as possible, so it would be over before his grandson's birthday party in the late summer, which he said he needed to attend. Whereupon, the judge had to schedule the trial for the summer. Though he indicated— confidentially to the two lawyers—some amusement at Catalano's confidence that, following the trial, he would be at liberty to attend a birthday party.

CONDON SAID he had heard that when Msgr. Gambino was first informed of the murder, he responded—as if involuntarily, under his breath, in a kind of half-tone—

one word: "Congilosi." But then immediately seeming to catch himself, as if realizing he had misspoken, and that his statement might be taken for an accusation he was not willing or prepared to make formally, did not further articulate his statement.

HE RELATED one remarkable incident. An incident contributing to his sense that there was something strange about this case, some subtle pressures in play. He said that early on, soon after he had been assigned to the case, he went to police headquarters, where his client was being questioned, and when he walked into the room where the questioning was taking place, who did he find grilling his client—trying to get him to confess—but the mayor. Mayor Sedita. He said he was stunned. He had no idea what to make of it.

ONE OF the things he said he remembered, there was extensive evidence and testimony about the ink used in the sign matching up with ink found in Catalano's apartment. He said it was Waterman's ink, an extremely common brand of ink that could be expected to be found in just about any home at that time. So that it was remarkable that the prosecution should have presented this bit of evidence as significant. Particularly since it had been virtually stipulated all around—based on other evidence and testimony—that Catalano had made the sign.

SOMETHING CONDON said several times—with some feeling—was that the police and prosecution had the newspaper writers "in their pockets." Police and prosecutors were regular information sources for journalists, and journalists provided essentially a public forum for the police and prosecutors, for their angle, their take, their bias, on whatever case or newsworthy matter. Which usually accorded with the bias of the newspaper audience, which tended to equate accused with guilty, and wanted an eye for an eye. Whereas, defense attorneys—partly because they were more varied from case to case, and so didn't get to deal with reporters on as regular a basis as their prosecutorial counterparts, but even more because they didn't supply the kind of accusatory information the newspapers preferred—lacked an equal or similar relationship with the press. "The newspaper reporters would know what was going on before the defense did," Condon said.

I TRIED to ask about the complicated business relative to Mrs. Congilosi's medical treatments, and whether she had fallen at home or at work. Whether all this had to do with trying to show or plant a seed of inference that her injuries were or might have been due to physical abuse by her husband. But Condon said that after so many years he was unable to recollect or reconstruct the trial strategies in such detail.

27

I LOCATED and contacted Carman Ball, the prosecutor, who later became Judge Ball. He was also retired and living in Florida, but also still had a residence in Western New York and came back from time to time. We met and talked at his home in Orchard Park, another suburb.

I said I had read the newspaper accounts of the murder and the trial, and with all due respect, I had to say I was skeptical of the police and prosecution theory that the old guy, Catalano, was pursuing the woman, and killed Father Belle because of Belle's what would have been legitimate interference in Catalano's nefarious project. And I said, given the differences in general attitudes between that time and the present—the way we thought of clergy in 1960 versus the way we might think of them in more recent times—that is, being more cognizant and conscious of their human fallibility—I was skeptical of the general sense that Father Belle was a holy innocent, and thus the "fanatic" theory, that therefore the murderer had to have been authentically crazy.

Ball said he could understand my point of view, but didn't concede it. He said, "We weren't able to make the case we wanted to make against Catalano." He said, "there were some things we were unable to establish." For example, he said he had heard from police that when Catalano drove Mrs. Congilosi and her son to his special school outside the city, on the way back they would stop at a motel.

REGARDING THE ballistics tests that determined the gun was a revolver not an automatic, I asked if in those days they really could tell from ballistics tests whether the gun was a revolver or automatic. How certain they could be of such information. Ball said he thought they could determine that, and the information would be fairly reliable, quite reliable, but not absolutely certain, he thought.

28.

I CONTACTED Buffalo Police Homicide Chief Joseph Riga, and asked if I could see the police file on the Father Belle murder. He said he would have his secretary look up the file and, "if that matter has been adjudicated," I would probably be able to look at the file.

I CONTACTED former Buffalo Police Chief Ralph Degenhart, who was Chief of Detectives at the time of the Msgr. O'Connor incident. I asked him if homosexuality was a factor in the O'Connor case. He said he couldn't talk about the case, since no arrest was ever made, and therefore the case was still open. He referred me to Chief Riga to ask if I could see the file.

I explained to Degenhart my real interest was in the Father Belle case. I asked him if he thought there could have been a homosexual connection in that case. He said he was not primarily involved in the Father Belle murder investigation, but knew of the case. But he said, no, there was no homosexual connection in the Belle case. He said Catalano was the murderer. He said Catalano had falsely accused Father Belle, then murdered him.

I TALKED to Chief Riga again six weeks or so after I had initially contacted him. He said his secretary was still looking for the Belle file, but hadn't found it yet. I told him in the meantime, since he and I had previously talked, I had talked to Degenhart and asked him about Msgr. O'Connor. I said Degenhart said he couldn't talk about the O'Connor case because it was still open, but had referred me to Riga to ask if I could see the file. I said I had asked Degenhart if there had been a homosexual connection in the O'Connor case. I said a priest had told me, or suggested, O'Connor was homosexual, and I was trying to find out if there was a homosexual connection between O'Connor and Belle. Riga asked when was the O'Connor murder. I told him his body was found in Scajaquada Creek on March 12, 1966. He said he would also look for the O'Connor file for me.

I called Riga again six or so weeks later, and asked if there was any progress in the search for the files. He said they hadn't found them yet, but were still looking. He said they were looking—or were going to be looking—in a basement storage area.

After several more months, I gave up hope of getting to look at any police files. Anyway, I had reason to believe the O'Connor file at least had been consigned to somebody's fireplace. Or maybe was at the bottom of the river. If so, I thought likely the Belle file was at the bottom of the river as well. Or consigned to somebody's fireplace.

THE NEWS update story on the O'Connor case—about the possibility of a cover-up in that case—said that in its preparation of the story, the *News* had filed a Freedom of Information Act request for police records on the matter. In response to which, the story said:

> Buffalo Police provided a redacted file...but large portions of it are missing. There are no reports written about the monsignor's body being found, or any reports on interviews conducted in the first two weeks after the body was found [on March 12, 1966]. The file contains 30 reports on interviews conducted by detectives between March 28 and May 3, 1966. There were no reports after that.

I TRIED to contact former Erie County Sheriff Michael Amico (who had been a Buffalo cop and investigator, and testified at the trial). I found his home address and wrote to him, but got no response.

29.

I WROTE to District Attorney Frank Clark, to ask if I could see his office's records on the Father Belle case. (I wouldn't have trusted the police records—which I wasn't getting to see anyway—but I thought I could possibly get all or most of the same records—duplicates perhaps—from the District Attorney's office.) After a long delay, I received a letter from the District Attorney's office saying they had no file on the Father Belle case, since no arrest was ever made in the case.

I wrote back that, in fact, an arrest had been made, and a trial conducted, resulting in an acquittal. Not hearing back from them, after two weeks or so I called and talked on the phone with a secretary in the office, who said all the files from that long ago had been disposed of. I said it was hard to believe the file could have been disposed of on a murder case only a few decades old, where some of the parties involved—including the murderer—might still be around. (I don't recall if I mentioned—but should have—that moreover the case was never solved. So it was still an open case.) She said, nonetheless, the file no longer existed.

30.

LATE IN the game, a friend—a lawyer—suggested I track down the court record on the trial. I had never heard of a court record. I didn't know what it was. What it would consist of.

I went to the County Court building, the Office of Criminal Records, and inquired if there was a file on the Father Belle case. The clerk hunted down the file. What it consisted of—in a single manila envelope—was three waivers of immunity—one for Mr. Congilosi, one for Mrs. Congilosi, and one for her sister, Mrs. Swier—relative to their grand jury testimonies. When witnesses testify before a grand jury, standard practice is that they sign a waiver of immunity. Otherwise their appearance as witnesses would automatically grant them immunity in the matter in question.

Nothing else in the envelope. Apparently, these were the only three witnesses that testified before the grand jury that indicted Catalano.

MR. CONGILOSI. The immediate first suspect. Who is questioned by the police, but not charged. And we never hear from him again. Though from time to time about him. According to trial testimony, a man of violent propensities—physically abusive of Mrs. Congilosi on at least one recorded occasion—and erratic. Who, according to his wife lived barricaded in the basement, with an ax and a gun. And threatened to kill Mrs. Congilosi on account of her supposedly having affairs with numerous men, including Father Belle. (Or maybe just his suspicion and mistrust about her possibly ever having an affair or affairs.) Whereby seemingly with a motive—even if paranoid—or maybe all the more so as paranoid—for killing Father Belle.

AND MRS. CONGILOSI. Whose story about Catalano's romantic pursuit of herself—a romantic project Catalano conceives Father Belle is interfering with via Father Belle's supposed own romantic relationship with Mrs. Congilosi, and threatens at various times and in various situations to kill Mrs. Congilosi, and her husband, and all their children, and Father Belle as well—a story readily accordant with the matter of the sign in the back of the church and the phone call to the pastor accusing Father Belle of some unspecified amorous misconduct—both pretty clearly Catalano's work—becomes the salient basis of the police and prosecution "fanatic" theory of the case, that whoever murdered Father Belle must have been a fanatic—a madman—on the premise that accusations against Father Belle had to be figments of the imagination of a madman, on the further premise that Father Belle was a saint on earth.

THE FACT that at other times—according to other trial testimony—Catalano was said to have said that Mrs. Congilosi was a good woman, but only that her husband was bad, and he wanted to kill him and marry her—the idea that on the one hand Catalano would accuse Mrs. Congilosi of multiple infidelity improprieties, while on the other hand he spoke well of her and even wanted to marry her— was thought not so much to undercut her story as to attest to Catalano's essential nuttiness, essential fanaticism.

*   *

ONE THING that seems clear—as if ultimately emerging from the miasma of trial testimony inconsistencies and implausibilities and contradictions into the clear light of day—is that, despite Mrs. Congilosi's reported avowal that she was happily married, she was not. That her relationship with her husband was not so much a relationship of love as of fear. Fear of his threats. As recounted in various witness testimonies. That he threatened to kill her—and maybe some or maybe all of their children—with an ax, no less.

Threats strangely similar to Catalano's in the bizarre and confusing story—or stories—in the newspaper accounts in January, ostensibly from Felicetta or other police source, but which he or they must have heard from Mrs. Congilosi—and then in Mrs. Congilosi's trial testimony— of street encounters with Catalano the evening before the murder and then some ten or twelve hours after the murder. When Catalano, armed with a gun, was said to have threatened to kill her and her whole family, including her husband and all their children.

*   *

I THINK Mrs. Congilosi made up her story—or essential key parts of the story—to deflect suspicion from her husband, whom she feared. And feared in particular the consequences if he were charged with the murder (even though that might have been the safest possible outcome for her). Her story that becomes the salient basis of the official theory of the case. It's basically just her story.

OR HERS and her sister's, Mrs. Swier's. Who would have understood and appreciated her sister's plight regarding the abusive and erratic husband—the catastrophe that could easily have ensued from that situation—and whose testimony—in a misconceived sisterly aid endeavor—was basically just another version of Mrs. Congilosi's story. About Catalano's romantic project regarding Mrs. Congilosi, and supposed grievance against Father Belle for his supposed interference in that project, with embellishment details about Catalano's threats—against Father Belle, in this case—and guns. Her added mention of Catalano accusing her sister of marital infidelity—much as long since reported in the newspapers in January—what Felicetta said Mr. Congilosi said Catalano had told him—seemed basically intended to confirm Catalano's "fanatic" character.

IN THE only other relevant testimony regarding Catalano's attitude toward Father Belle, and the nature and substance of his threats, Mrs. Congilosi's daughter, Phyllis Congilosi, testified that Catalano threatened only Mr. Congilosi. And her fiancé, Timothy McLaren, testified that Catalano made threats against Mr. Congilosi and some unnamed priests—threats McLaren said Catalano seemed serious about, but that McLaren seemed to consider bluster pure and simple. "You are watching too many television programs."

BUT THEN Mr. Congilosi's story, too—the story he told police, about Catalano accusing Mrs. Congilosi of having affairs with several men including Father Belle—that was a made-up story, too. (So pity the poor police and prosecutors, having to try to figure out a murder incident working from three—though really two—different—though partially interdependent—made-up stories. But not pity too much. Because at the same time the police and prosecutors were making up a story—their story—as well.)

*   *

WHY MR. Congilosi's story—that Catalano had accused Mrs. Congilosi of having affairs with several men including Father Belle—was made up is that, based on all other relevant testimony—that is, other than that of Mrs. Congilosi and her sister, Mrs. Swier, whose made-up stories, or story, incorporated this element of Mr. Congilosi's story—Catalano would hardly have said that about a woman he otherwise always spoke highly of and even wanted to marry. Apparently he did want to replace Mr. Congilosi in the paternal role in that family, but essentially, it seems, to rescue Mrs. Congilosi and the rest of the family from a vicious and obnoxious husband and father. And legitimately marry Mrs. Congilosi—in testimony there was no suggestion of an extramarital affair, as there had seemed to be—by innuendo at least—in the newspapers in January, and no doubt residually thereafter in the popular imagination—once she was free to marry, following termination of her present marriage. Termination—it must be admitted—possibly by way of Catalano killing Mr. Congilosi, per Phyllis Congilosi's testimony.

Or per her fiancé Timothy McLaren's testimony, shooting Mr. Congilosi "in the cellar of his house," and also "those priests," and "that priest." Which McLaren considered bluster. Whereas what McLaren said Catalano said of Mrs. Congilosi was simply that she was "a good woman."

Phyllis Congilosi also said she heard Catalano tell Mr. Congilosi: "'You don't deserve your good family and good children. If I were in your place I'd be very happy.'" And that Catalano told her, "he wanted to take her father's place because her mother 'was a good woman and my father didn't appreciate her.'"

In cross-examining Mrs. Swier, Condon asked if Catalano had ever said he wanted to have an affair with Mrs. Congilosi. Mrs. Swier: "No." Condon: "He said only that he wanted to marry her?" Mrs. Swier: "Yes."

AND WHY would Mr. Congilosi make up his story? About Catalano telling him about his wife's supposed infidelity with several men, including Father Belle. No doubt in an attempt to excuse—as if to excuse—his brutal treatment of his wife the police were then questioning him about. But also to discredit and disparage Father Belle, whom he would have detested for his interference in his—Congilosi's—domestic affairs, as in the present instance in particular, in which Father Belle intervened in a family fight in which Mr. Congilosi had struck Mrs. Congilosi, and told Mrs. Congilosi she didn't have to put up with such treatment from her husband. And called the police, whereupon Mr. Congilosi was taken in for questioning.

Possibly also detested Father Belle for ongoing pastoral counseling of Mrs. Congilosi and likely counseling advisement that she did not have to continue to submit to physical and mental abusive treatment from Mr. Congilosi.

AND WHY think Mrs. Congilosi's elaborate, complicated story was made-up—not the part about Catalano wanting to marry her, but about Catalano's threats against her and her whole family, and against Father Belle for his supposed interference in Catalano's romantic project—the reason to think these parts were made up—and specifically to deflect from Mr. Congilosi—is that the supposed Catalano threats so precisely mimic the threats we know more credibly—from various trial testimony—Mr. Congilosi directed at Mrs. Congilosi—to kill her and some or all of their children.

AS WELL as that the gist basis of Catalano's alleged grievance against Father Belle—interference in Catalano's romantic project—is precisely the gist basis of Mr. Congilosi's grievance against Father Belle—interference in his—Mr. Congilosi's—domestic affairs.

AND THEN that apparent inconsistency in the early and later editions *News* stories about the supposed confrontation with Catalano ten or twelve hours after the murder, when he allegedly displayed a gun and threatened Mrs. Congilosi. The early edition story notes that the confrontation occurred when Mr. Congilosi was not at home, while the later edition story says it occurred on the street. If it occurred on the street, why is it relevant that Mr. Congilosi was not at home at the time? Because the time when the street confrontation supposedly occurred would have been when Mr. Congilosi was at the police station being questioned as a suspect. Indicating what would have been foremost on Mrs. Congilosi's mind in fabricating her story. The possibility that Mr. Congilosi might be charged with murder. And in that eventuality her fear—maybe not entirely rational, but nonetheless vivid, in a case with a violent and abusive spouse—for herself, her family, her domestic situation.

MRS. CONGILOSI was not a particularly imaginative—in the sense of inventive—storyteller. But a rather transparent one. Her story—including the timing of the story—precisely reflects her real issues, real fears, which were fundamentally of a domestic nature, regarding Mr. Congi-losi. His threats.

*   *

AND THE police story—the official theory of the case—that the killing had to have been the work of a fanatic, a madman. Why the police story would have been made up was to avert scandal. To Father Belle, to Holy Cross Church, to the Catholic Church in general. An unofficial goal and objective of the police and other civil authori-ties—in this case stretching seemingly even to the mayor's office—but not an uncommon practice at the time rela-tive to matters connected to the Church. As in the Father O'Connor case. Or the regular police practice of turning over priests caught in some illegal activity or compromis-ing situation to the Masked Marvel priest for a good beat-ing in lieu of criminal charges and procedures. Or most egregiously, relative to the plethora of priest sexual abuse instances lately brought to light after being concealed for decades by Church authorities. Many or most of the abuse instances were likely somehow concealed also from—and thus unknown to—the police and civil authorities. But entirely so? Nobody among the police or relevant civil officials knew or heard or observed or suspected anything of the widespread pattern of clergy sexual abuse crimes over decades? Crimes the Church authorities regularly adjudicated merely by transferring the offending priest to a different parish (and new roster of potential victims).

The police and civil authorities had absolutely no notion or suspicion of this long-term pattern? It is hardly credible. It is not credible.

BUT THE police and prosecutors in the Father Belle case were from start to finish either in flagrant—though covert—collaboration with Church authorities—in a mutual endeavor at all costs to avoid scandal regarding Father Belle, and thus regarding the Church as a whole—or the police and prosecutors were quietly so much under the thumb and in the pocket of the Church—of the Church's political clout, however it might be manifested, however it operated—that they did it on their own.

*   *

I DON'T know what the sign in the back of the church and the phone call to the pastor were in reference to. What impropriety or indiscretion Catalano was accusing Father Belle of.

Possibly homosexual activity, but seemingly rather an affair with a woman, given the wording on the sign "la namorata" (properly la innamorata—or better l'innamorata—a lover, but the feminine grammatical gender indicating female actual gender).

But not likely Mrs. Congilosi, given the high regard Catalano clearly had for Mrs. Congilosi by all credible accounts, and the extremely questionable nature of the various accounts and allegations—including allegations of allegations—of romantic connection between Father Belle and Mrs. Congilosi.

But whatever the sign and phone messages had reference to, possibly that was what the police and civil authorities—on behalf of the Church—were at pains to cover up. Which could have been scandalous if it were made public.

Or possibly it was the alleged affair with Mrs. Congilosi they wished to cover up. Not actual affair, that is, but just serious allegation of such. (Versus an absurdist component of a fabricated story intended to demonstrate and expose—as the source of such a preposterous notion—a madman.) Which also would have been scandalous if it were made public. Which surely it would have been—made public—if Mr. Congilosi was ever charged with the murder. At the trial at least. What Mr. Congilosi would have testified he had reported to the police some weeks prior to the murder. (In which case perhaps essentially conceding that he had committed the murder—which given a sufficiently strong prosecution case against him might have been a gratuitous admission—but by way of contending that he had a rational motive for committing the murder. Which the jury—possibly an all-male jury, as happened in the Catalano trial—might have felt some sympathy with. As a mitigating factor at least.)

BUT I did understand why I didn't understand. Why the case from the beginning was so confusing, baffling. Because I wasn't supposed to understand. For the sake of the cover-up—as the mechanism of the cover-up—the theory of the case was that you couldn't understand it. It didn't make sense. The crime was the work of a madman. The work of a fanatic.

BUT THEN that they would offer a scapegoat—an old guy, semi-literate, who couldn't or wouldn't properly defend himself—that was beyond unconscionable. Not just shield the guilty, but if required, persecute the innocent. Whatever, to avoid scandal for the Church. Protect the institution.

BUT PRECISELY on the pattern of the years and decades Church practice of cover-up of clergy sex abuse. Minimal to no concern about victims, individuals. Total concern for the reputation of the Church, including clergy perpetrators of felony crimes. In ultimately a collaboration project between civil and Church authorities.

—30—

www.ingramcontent.com/pod-product-compliance
Lightning Source LLC
Chambersburg PA
CBHW030018290326
41934CB00005B/391